D1611023

Safer Beaches

Planning, Design, and Operation

Tom Griffiths, EdD

Human Kinetics

Library of Congress Cataloging-in-Publication Data

Griffiths, Tom, 1949-
  Safer beaches : planning, design, and operation / Tom Griffiths.
      p. cm.
  Includes bibliographical references and index.
  ISBN-13: 978-0-7360-8646-2 (hard cover)
  ISBN-10: 0-7360-8646-3 (hard cover)
  1. Beaches--Recreational use--Planning. 2. Beaches--Management. 3. Coastal zone
management. 4. Swimming--Management. 5. Beaches--Safety measures. 6. Swimming--Safety
measures. I. Title.
  GV191.67.W3G75 2011
  333.7844--dc22

                              2011011684

  ISBN-10: 0-7360-8646-3 (print)
  ISBN-13: 978-0-7360-8646-2 (print)

Permission notices for interior photographs in this book can be found on page vii.

The web addresses cited in this text were current as of April 19, 2011, unless otherwise noted.

Acquisitions Editors: Jill White and Gayle Kassing, PhD; **Developmental Editor:** Bethany J. Bentley; **Assistant Editor:** Derek Campbell; **Copyeditor:** Patricia MacDonald; **Indexer:** Sharon Duffy; **Permission Manager:** Dalene Reeder; **Graphic Designer:** Nancy Rasmus; **Graphic Artists:** Nancy Rasmus and Denise Lowry; **Cover Designer:** Bob Reuther; **Photographers (cover):** Tom Griffiths (top and bottom middle photos), Robert E. Ogoreuc (bottom left and right photos); **Photo Production Manager:** Jason Allen; **Art Manager:** Kelly Hendren; **Associate Art Manager:** Alan L. Wilborn; **Illustrations:** Courtesy of Clarion Safety Systems, all rights reserved; p. 3 adapted from NOAA; **Printer:** Sheridan Books

Printed in the United States of America   10 9 8 7 6 5 4 3 2 1

The paper in this book is certified under a sustainable forestry program.

Human Kinetics
Website: www.HumanKinetics.com

United States: Human Kinetics, P.O. Box 5076, Champaign, IL 61825-5076
800-747-4457
e-mail: humank@hkusa.com

Canada: Human Kinetics, 475 Devonshire Road Unit 100, Windsor, ON N8Y 2L5
800-465-7301 (in Canada only)
e-mail: info@hkcanada.com

Europe: Human Kinetics, 107 Bradford Road, Stanningley, Leeds LS28 6AT, United Kingdom
+44 (0) 113 255 5665
e-mail: hk@hkeurope.com

Australia: Human Kinetics, 57A Price Avenue, Lower Mitcham, South Australia 5062
08 8372 0999
e-mail: info@hkaustralia.com

New Zealand: Human Kinetics, P.O. Box 80, Torrens Park, South Australia 5062
0800 222 062
e-mail: info@hknewzealand.com

E4926

Contents

Preface

According to some estimates, more than 200 million Americans travel to the beach each year. The beaches they visit vary tremendously, from river to lake to ocean beaches. Whether it is the attraction of the magical blend of sun, sand, and water; the variety of flora and fauna; or the rising and setting of the sun and moon reflecting on the water's surface, the beach is a major attraction to multitudes.

Although millions of people enjoy relaxing, swimming, and playing at the beach, there are few resources that comprehensively address how to manage these recreational gems efficiently, safely, and affordably without sacrificing beach users' enjoyment. The United States Lifesaving Association (USLA) has provided an open-water lifeguarding manual that outlines safely guarding swimming beaches. In 1999, I authored *Better Beaches* for the National Recreation and Park Association (NRPA) to address some areas that USLA did not, such as the aesthetic qualities of beaches, unguarded beaches, and adopt-a-beach programs. But since 1999, few if any management resources have been added to the recreational beach arena. *Safer Beaches* is an attempt to increase awareness and provide new information for those managing and guarding beaches. Balancing safety and enjoyment is the backbone of this book.

Safer Beaches hopes to address not only those who work at beaches but also those who visit them, particularly those who bring groups to beaches, whether they be from schools, churches, or other organizations. This book will help beachgoers maximize their experience. Finally, for those administrators either creating new beaches or improving existing ones, information for funding sources and partnerships found within these pages will certainly be beneficial. Whereas other water texts address safety solely through lifeguarding techniques, this book examines increasing safety on guarded and unguarded beaches and emphasizes educating the public in addition to warning and regulating them.

Rather than tell the reader exactly how beaches should be maintained and supervised, this text provides a smorgasbord of helpful tips and techniques from beaches around the world. Although *Safer Beaches* focuses on an American audience, it borrows beach practices from around the world; family meeting places is just one example of a European safety practice that should be emulated here in the United States. As you will see, many of the photographs found on the pages were taken in other countries. This book attempts to combine the most important aspects of beach design, water safety, and water quality all in one reference book. Once you have completed this book, it would be a splendid idea to visit several well-maintained beaches to get a firsthand look at what it takes to run a beach.

Because lifeguarding relies totally on the human senses to protect others, a myriad of strategies for helping lifeguards be more vigilant are offered. Unlike many other water safety texts, the recommendations for increasing lifeguard effectiveness come from a variety of sources.

Safer Beaches also explores new areas of study. Chapters on funding, above-water structures (docks and piers), and beaches and waterfronts *not* intended for swimming are included. The sections on the new signage standards should raise the standard of care in that vitally important area. Risk management and accessibility are also important topics that are traditional areas of study.

Safer Beaches was written primarily as a management tool. Hopefully, you will find the secrets of success for many of the world's beaches. However, since beaches are so unique, it is difficult to come up with standards that all beaches must follow. Applying the information presented in this book to your beach will definitely help, however. This book is an essential addition to the shelves of beach managers, lifeguards, administrators, and beach enthusiasts because of the current lack of information specifically written on the topic of safe beach management. Until now, much of the information used by beach managers came from swimming pool and water park resources. Because it is unfair and unrealistic to apply swimming pool and water park standards to an open-water setting, *Safer Beaches* is more important than ever before.

Credits

Photos on pp. 1, 2, 6, 9, 15, 19, 21, 23, 29, 59, 60, 62, 64, 71, 77, 79, 80, 83, 97, 104, 109, 124 courtesy of Tom Griffiths.

Photos on pp. 11, 13, 49, 69, 81, 85, 112 courtesy of Robert E. Ogoreuc.

Photos on pp. 25, 27 courtesy of Mobi-mat, www.mobi-mat.com.

Photo on p. 31 courtesy of B. Chris Brewster, San Diego, CA.

Photo on p. 33 © Brent Reeves.

Photos on pp. 41, 45, 46 courtesy of Clarion Safety Systems. All rights reserved.

Photos on pp. 48, 50, 87 courtesy of Pat Kilroy, Director, City of Lake Elsinore, CA.

Photos on pp. 67, 75, 94 courtesy of Rachel Griffiths.

Photo on p. 91 by Jennifer Zeigler, courtesy of State College PA magazine.

Photos on pp. 52, 106 courtesy of Brenda Culler, Ohio Department of Natural Resource Office of Coastal Management.

Photo on p. 116 courtesy of Cathy Sheder, CampAquatics.

Photo on p. 121 © Human Kinetics.

Logo on p. 121 courtesy of United States Lifesaving Association.

Beach Types and Hazards

1

Vive la difference! Because beaches are so unique with many advantages and disadvantages, beach managers need to know how to best educate beachgoers so their visitors can safely enjoy their beaches. Knowing the demographics of those using the beach along with the idiosyncrasies of the beach will provide for optimal and safe recreational use. This chapter helps you attain this goal so the beach experience will be memorable.

No two beaches are alike. Many beaches do, however, have some similarities. When considering all different beaches, perhaps it is best to establish three major categories for better discussion: surf beaches, flat-water beaches, and river beaches. Regardless of what type of beach is maintained, each has unique hazards that must be known and identified. Reducing conflicts between diverse user groups and warning guests of hidden hazards are of the utmost importance.

Surf Beaches

Approximately 71 percent of the earth's surface is covered by oceans. This much water produces 375,000 miles (600,000 km) of coastline throughout the world, with 13,000 miles (21,000 km) of coastline found in the United States. The end result is that the world is blessed with hundreds of thousands of beaches for people of all walks of life to enjoy. Many of these beaches have varying amounts of surf and tides. Although often thought to be ocean beaches exclusively, surf beaches also include other large bodies of water with waves and currents and "great waters," including such water bodies as the Great Lakes and the Gulf of Mexico. Wind-generated waves affect sand, rocks, and corals to produce beach sand along with river sediment deposits. The forces of nature produce dynamic and diverse surf beaches that are not only aesthetically pleasing, meditative in nature, and enjoyable but also sometimes dangerous, containing inherent risks and hazards.

Surf beach dangers can vary from very slight to very severe depending on environmental conditions. These dangers include but are not limited to high surf and rip currents; dangerous marine life varying with locality; geological hazards such as rocks, cliffs, reefs, and drop-offs; and pollution

Surf beaches are exciting but can also be the most dangerous. Large waves, strong currents, and rocky shorelines add to the thrill of the beach experience, but accidents can happen without proper training.

from industrial, agricultural, and urban sources. Well-known geographer Bernard Nietschmann maintains that the severity of beach hazards depends on three interacting factors:

1. The prevalence and severity of hazards
2. The knowledge and experience of the surf beach user
3. The presence or absence of professional lifeguards

A more comprehensive discussion of the intricacies of surf beaches can be found in the manual *Open Water Lifesaving*, published by the United States Lifesaving Association (Brewster 2003).

Rip Currents

As dangerous as they are, rip currents may be the surf beach hazard beachgoers understand the least. However, beachgoers must be aware of and knowledgeable about rip currents more than any other hazard. According to the United States Lifesaving Association, approximately 80 percent of all ocean rescues are the result of rip currents. These are localized inshore currents produced by local conditions and should not be referred to as *tides*. Perhaps it is best to describe rip currents in simple terms: as fast-flowing streams or rivers running out away from the beach and beyond the breaker line. Rip currents are relatively narrow but extremely strong and forceful, and they can

pull swimmers and waders away from the beach at an alarming rate. Even the strongest of competitive swimmers cannot beat a rip current by swimming against it. Fortunately, rip currents are easily dealt with by swimming parallel to the beach to remove oneself from the current's grasp. Unfortunately, when people find themselves in the clutches of a rip current, they do exactly what they should *not* do—they attempt to swim back to the beach, directly into the stronger current. Panic sets in quickly, and drowning follows. Another good thing about rip currents is that they are typically very short lived. Although some rip currents can be more than a quarter mile (.4 km) long, most are not more than a few hundred yards or meters. Strong swimmers, surfers, lifeguards, and scuba divers actually use rip currents as a shortcut beyond the surf zone.

It is important to understand how a rip current is born. When wind and waves grow in size and intensity, water pushes and piles up on the beach. After running up the beach, the water seeks its own level by rushing quickly back into the ocean. The strong returning rush of water will often follow underwater channels and troughs on the ocean floor, flow between sandbars, or arise where two opposing longshore currents meet. Rip currents may also arise alongside jetties. In general, the greater the wind, wave, and surf activity, the stronger the rip currents (see figure 1.1).

Although rip currents do display some telltale signs, they are difficult for most tourists and

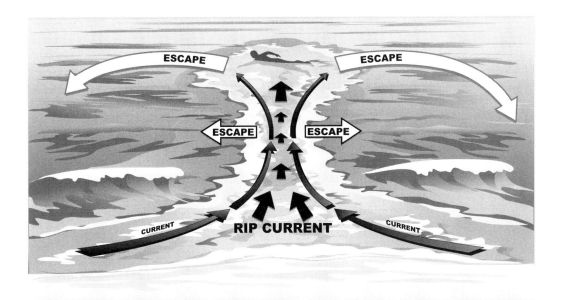

FIGURE 1.1 Although a rip current is extremely strong, fortunately it is both narrow and relatively short lived. The key to surviving a rip is to relax and either ride it out or swim parallel to shore, where you will soon be free of its grasp.

day-trippers to detect. Because only the most seasoned beachgoers, lifeguards, and surfers easily recognize rip currents, they should be considered a hidden hazard to guests and therefore should be signed aggressively. Beach warning flags may also help educate guests if they can be changed in a timely fashion. Detecting rip currents calls for an astute observation of the seascape. Rip currents usually display irregularities on the surface of the water. Typically, these surface irregularities show subtle yet significant traces in a perpendicular path away from the shoreline. A line of small, choppy waves; a line of discolored muddy, murky water; or a line of foam and bubbles going out away from the beach and through the surf zone are perhaps the most reliable signs of a rip current. These signs exist in the narrow, strong neck of the rip and quickly dissipate once the neck dissipates in the head of the current.

Again, although these markers are easy to observe by some, they are readily missed by many. Once caught in a rip current, the unsuspecting victim should attempt to remain calm and work on rhythmic breathing. Two good choices are available when caught in a rip current. One is to simply float and tread water and ride out the rip current beyond the breaker line. Once the rip current dissipates, the swimmer can move slowly parallel to the beach and away from the rip. The other option is to simply swim parallel to shore immediately following the grasp of the rip current without waiting for the rip to pull the swimmer too far from shore. If the swim back to the shoreline is lengthy, the swimmer should wave for assistance. Tragically, swimmers learn about rip currents only when it is too late, and some never live to tell about them.

Surf Zone

Undoubtedly, it's the surf that attracts so many people to our coastlines. The surf zone refers to the wave action between the shoreline and the waves breaking farthest from it. Surf is composed of wind-generated waves. As the wind increases, so do the height and strength of the waves. Big surf attracts many avid water sports enthusiasts, but it also brings with it a myriad of risks and hazards.

Plunging Waves

Plunging waves are produced by a combination of strong waves and a steeply inclined beach. These waves are characterized by their height and force

and are distinguishable in that the breaking crest of the wave curls over and forward to the wave's base without touching the face of the wave. The more enticing the waves are for surfers, the more dangerous they are. Warning beach flags can be especially useful as wave height and strength change, but again, flags must be updated in a timely fashion as the surf conditions change. Entering and exiting the surf zone through large plunging waves can be tricky and even dangerous at times.

Shorebreaks

When plunging waves seem to come from nowhere and break directly on the beach rather than farther out in the surf zone, it is called a shorebreak. This wave action can literally pick people up and rotate them onto their heads, causing severe head and neck injuries. Shorebreak waves can knock people off their feet and then drag them back into the surf with their resulting backwash. Whenever a surf beach is characterized by shorebreak, beachgoers must be warned.

Spilling Waves

Spilling waves tend to be more user friendly and safer for waders, novice swimmers, and beginning surfers. Spilling waves simply roll up through the surf zone and onto the beach without breaking or crashing and most often occur at beaches with gradual bottom slopes. When waves break on the beach, water moves up the beach, known as a wash, swash, or uprush. Conversely, when this same water returns to the ocean, it is called backwash. Backwash can be strong and problematic, but it is not the mysterious undertow that really does not exist. The taller the waves and the steeper the beach, the more severe backwash becomes.

Surging Waves

Surging waves neither curl nor break but simply and quickly rise and fall. The sudden rise and fall of a huge mass of water can cause real problems for unsuspecting visitors. These types of waves are most problematic around rocky coastlines, piers, jetties, and some steep beaches. The powerful rise and fall of surging waves can quickly and abruptly lift people off their feet and deposit them on rocks, and people have been killed by severe head trauma as a result. When it comes to surging waves, the old Hawaiian saying applies: "Never turn your back on the sea!"

Nearshore Current

Waves breaking at and around the beach create current systems known as inshore, or nearshore, currents. Longshore, or littoral, currents are produced when waves roll into the beach at an angle rather than straight on or parallel to the beach. Longshore currents are not particularly dangerous but do move up or down the beach and carry swimmers and waders with them. Although these currents don't directly affect the safety of guests in the water, they can pose a hazard by moving people away from family and friends, making it more difficult to track swimmers and causing some people—particularly children—to get lost on the beach. When two opposing longshore currents meet, they can produce rip currents. Likewise, rip currents can be created between sandbars. Sandbars are often attractions for swimmers and waders, especially during low tides, but when people step off a sandbar to return to the beach, conditions may have changed so that the gap between sandbars becomes a conduit for water rushing out to sea. These inshore currents escaping between sandbars can create deeper, fast-moving water called rip feeder channels and can be especially dangerous.

Dangerous Marine Life

Although larger marine life-forms in the ocean with notorious reputations can scare beachgoers, in reality, sharks, killer whales, barracuda, moray eels, and stingrays rarely pose a threat to beach visitors. While worrying about the larger "monsters" in the sea, beachgoers are more likely to be annoyed or slightly injured by smaller, more innocuous creatures such as jellyfish, hydroids, and corals. For more comprehensive information on dangerous marine life, please consult USLA. The following brief discussion of dangerous marine life is broken down into the mechanism of injury to the beachgoer by the organism.

Organisms That Abrade, Lacerate, or Puncture

These organisms include barnacles, hard corals, sea urchins, stingrays, and cone shells. Except for cone shells, most of these creatures do not inject poison but rather inflict dirty wounds that are easily infected and hard to heal. Before entering the water, beachgoers should check with local authorities and lifeguards to ascertain if any of these organisms can be found in the water and, if so, how to prevent injury. Water shoes and protective water clothing may be recommended in certain areas. Cleaning the puncture wound completely and consulting a physician is highly recommended.

Poisonous Fish

Poisonous fish do in fact exist in our oceans, but fortunately, they are mostly found in remote, unpopulated areas. Some of the most notorious venomous fish include scorpionfish, stonefish, zebra lionfish, and weever fish. When a poisonous fish inflicts a wound, immediate cleaning and soaking in very hot water is beneficial. A physician should be consulted as soon as possible to prescribe antibiotics, but in the meantime, soaking the wound while immobilizing the victim and treating for shock is probably the best course of action.

Organisms That Sting

Ocean organisms that sting include jellyfish and hydroids such as fire corals and the Portuguese man-of-war. Of marine life injuries, stinging injuries are the most common by far. The stinging organisms are characterized by spring-loaded stinging cells called nematocysts. These stinging cells fire reflexively when touched, whether the organism is dead or alive. Most stinging injuries are typically more annoying than debilitating. The long tentacles of a Portuguese man-of-war, however, with their thousands of nematocysts, can inflict serious harm to swimmers, even respiratory arrest. Any material worn in the water can help prevent stings, including T-shirts, panty hose, and the ever-popular and fashionable Lycra stinger suits. Treating stings with vinegar, rubbing alcohol, baking soda, and meat tenderizer all seem to offer varying degrees of relief, and scraping the stingers from the skin with a credit card can also be helpful. When stinging organisms are prevalent at a beach, visitors should be warned both at the beach and through various media outlets.

Organisms That Bite

Biting marine organisms include sharks, moray eels, sea snakes, barracuda, and schooling fish. Fortunately, encounters with these potential biters are rare. If swimmers are bitten by any form of marine life, timely emergency medical care is critical. Stopping the bleeding, immobilizing the victim, and treating for shock are important responsibilities of the first responders.

Confined Flat-Water Beaches

Flat-water beaches are typical of inland lakes, ponds, bays, and sounds. Great waters such as the Great Lakes can be flat-water lakes at times but can easily become surf beaches as the weather changes. Flat-water lakes with less than 500 acres (200 hectares) of water surface are considered small, whereas flat-water lakes with more than 500 acres of water surface are considered large. When swimming is allowed, the designated swimming areas are significantly smaller than the entire body of water.

Although flat-water beaches may appear to be tranquil and safe, many of the hazards are hidden to the casual observer and pose potentially serious problems for unsuspecting lifeguards and patrons.

Lifeguard Inexperience

Lifeguards at many flat-water beaches, particularly the smaller beaches, are younger, less experienced, and often not supervised as frequently. Flat-water lifeguards also tend to be part-time seasonal employees rather than full-time employees with benefits. This differs from surf beaches where older, more mature, and experienced professional lifeguards typically guard the shoreline. Surf lifeguards are often full-time employees with benefits.

Flat-water beaches, like this one in New Jersey, can be reflective, both literally and figuratively. But don't let the serenity of the flat-water beach fool you. Flat-water beaches can be deceptively dangerous, with hidden hazards such as sudden drop-offs, aquatic plant life, underwater obstructions, and a lack of clarity.

Swimmer Inexperience

Generally speaking, surf beaches tend to attract stronger swimmers, whereas flat-water beaches entice more novice swimmers and families with younger children. Even though flat-water beaches appear to be less hazardous than surf beaches, the clientele they attract may be more at risk because of their more limited swimming ability. Overconfidence and a false sense of security can be problematic for guests and lifeguards alike at flat, freshwater beaches. Surf beaches often contain saltwater, which makes swimmers more buoyant and results in a slight margin of safety. Freshwater does not offer as much buoyancy to swimmers.

Ocean and other great-water lifeguards appreciate the hazards of waves and currents and therefore possess a higher level of vigilance, knowing that swimmers will encounter problems in the water. Novice swimmers approaching the surf zone will be less likely to attempt to negotiate large waves and as a result remain closer to shore. Flat-water beaches, on the other hand, do not possess many obvious hazards such as tall waves and strong currents. The flat, gentle waters of the flat-water beach can result in monotony for the lifeguards and overconfidence in parents and children, thus producing a recipe for disaster. B. Chris Brewster, president of the United States Lifesaving Association, believes surf separates strong swimmers from weaker swimmers, but flat-water beaches have no means of distinguishing between abilities. A wader at a flat-water beach could be an Olympic swimmer or a potential drownee, but the lifeguard on duty will not know this until the wader attains water above his head, and then it can be too late. As a result, everyone in a flat-water beach environment is a potential victim, and the drowning scenario can begin quickly and quietly.

When swimmers or waders slip beneath the surface of any open-water environment, they become extremely difficult to locate and retrieve in a timely fashion, even by the most competent lifeguards. Once below the surface of the water, a victim may not fully recover from a submersion of as little as two minutes. It must be remembered that many flat-water beach guests often equate this specific open-water environment to a swimming pool or a water park. This is simply not the case because of limited visibility, vegetation, and uneven and irregular bottoms. A submerged victim in the open water is at greater peril than a submerged victim in a clear-water swimming pool, although both are truly at risk.

Water Clarity and Water Pollution

Although poor water clarity (visibility) alone cannot cause drowning, it certainly makes it more difficult to search for, recover, and resuscitate a victim in a timely fashion. As more people enter the swimming area, the water clarity often worsens. Because poor water clarity is such a contributing factor in flat-water beach drownings, great care must be taken to keep all swimmers and waders safely on the surface.

Bottom Conditions and Water Depth

Irregular bottom contours and poor visibility combine to produce hidden hazardous conditions at many flat-water beaches. Holes, sudden drop-offs, and troughs can all be disastrous for waders and weaker swimmers. For those who are weaker swimmers, uneven beach bottoms in particular can unexpectedly lead to distress and disappearance in the designated swimming area. Unfortunately, stepping into underwater depressions or suddenly deep water is not uncommon in flat-water beach areas. Walking in chest- to shoulder-depth water can be catastrophic for many waders and novice swimmers when they encounter a sudden and unexpected change in depth. When a swimmer or wader suddenly finds herself over her head in water with limited visibility, disaster may result quickly. Another problem with the bottom in flat-water areas is that without waves and currents, there can be a buildup of sediment, causing significantly slippery slopes. Particularly in lakes or ponds slick with algae growth and mud, unsuspecting waders can slide into deep water. Other bottom hazards include stumps, rocks, and other obstructions that can trip waders. These underwater hazards can also severely injure those who dive headfirst into the designated swimming area.

Flotation Devices

A greater variety of flotation devices are used at flat-water beaches as opposed to surf beaches. Weaker swimmers and younger swimmers tend to use these devices at flat-water beaches, where not much skill is needed to utilize them. Compounding the problem is the wide availability of these devices at low prices. Swimmers who fall off flotation devices may not be noticed, and rescue and recovery become more difficult in open water when submersion goes undetected. If a nonswimmer slips off a device in deep water, he may not be rescued in time.

Deep-Water Floating Features

With the advent of water parks, flat-water beaches often add floating features that are fun and exciting to use in order to compete for guests. These may include rafts; blobs; water trampolines; icebergs; and inflatable slides, docks, and obstacle courses.

Floating Rafts

Many flat-water beaches are characterized by a shallow-water wading area and a deep-water area with floating docks or rafts that often contain diving boards and slides on top. Although deep-water rafts were popular and still are common, they are no longer considered as safe as once thought, unless aggressively regulated and guarded. Just as 10-foot (3 m) diving boards are becoming obsolete for safety reasons, so should deep-water amenities in lakes if they are not properly supervised. Deep-water rafts attract weaker swimmers, just as black diamond expert slopes attract intermediate and novice downhill skiers.

Blobs, Water Trampolines, and Other Inflatables

Blobs are both unique and fun for those visiting flat-water beaches. Typically, a heavier participant jumps from a tower onto a large floating blob to eject a lighter participant sitting on the blob. Water trampolines are inflatable structures that are several feet high and often a dozen or more feet wide. A participant jumps on the trampoline or uses the bounce from the trampoline to propel himself into the water. Inflatable icebergs, climbing walls, slides, and obstacle courses are floating devices of various sizes, shapes, and heights. Collisions with other people and the bottom are unfortunately common with the use of all these inflatable devices.

Rope Swings and Zip Lines

Rope swings and zip lines can also be fun, but they are quite a bit more challenging, requiring a good deal of upper arm strength. Serious injury can result from premature drops from the lines into shallow water or, worse yet, onto land.

Aquatic Life

Although freshwater aquatic plants, animals, reptiles, and fish rarely cause problems for swimmers, they can induce fear and panic in some, which can indirectly lead to drowning. Perhaps the best example of a tiny innocuous creature creating panic in a swimmer is the freshwater leech. Likewise, freshwater weeds rarely cause problems for swimmers, but detecting them seems to instill fear in some people. Shells are another potential hazard. They appear harmless lying in the sand but can act like razor blades on bare feet.

Weeds

Weeds and other plant life tend to grow in the absence of waves and currents, typical of flat-water beaches. Weeds and plants can be particularly troublesome if a swimmer believes she can become entangled in them. Although most weeds are not capable of stopping or holding a swimmer in the water, if a swimmer *thinks* the weeds can be a problem, they probably will be.

Leeches

Leeches are ugly, bloodsucking worms that can attach to swimmers without letting go. They are found in just about all freshwater environments. Although leeches are not dangerous and are used for medicinal purposes in some cultures, they can cause panic and shock in some people that can require medical attention. Professional assistance is often needed to remove them from the skin.

Snapping Turtles

Although many different species of turtles are found in fresh water, only snapping turtles are a potential threat to swimmers and waders, and even then, only when they are trapped or cornered. Snapping turtles can grow to impressive sizes, and swimmers and waders should be warned not to provoke them. Again, although snapping turtles rarely bite humans, the anticipation of being bitten is worse than the reality, and stress and panic may result.

Freshwater Mussels

Freshwater mussels can also be a real problem by cutting the bottoms of bare feet, particularly half shells from dead mussels. Where freshwater mussels are present, guests should be encouraged to wear water shoes, and lifeguards and park rangers should be prepared to offer first aid for lacerated feet. Lacerations caused by mussels can quickly become infected if not cleaned and treated properly.

Alligators, Reptiles, and Lizards

These wildlife can be a hazard to humans. Since being protected by a Florida law in 1962, alligators have been on the rise in the southeastern United States, especially in major river drainage basins and large warm-water lakes. Although the risk of alligators biting humans is extremely low, it does exist. Swimmers and waders should not enter waters that contain alligators, particularly during the evening when reptiles normally feed. Just as important, feeding alligators should be banned. Anyone bitten by an alligator should seek immediate attention from a physician.

River Beaches

River beaches are a different breed of beach. They have incessant flow and current that can pose significant hazards to beachgoers. Perhaps river beaches can be best described as a hybrid, somewhere between a flat-water beach and a surf beach. River beaches are typically less common than surf and flat-water beaches because of the incessant current and the unreliable height of the river. When planned properly, however, river

Rivers are incessant and deceiving; they don't stop or slow down, regardless of who gets caught in their currents. Although they often look calm, they can be very powerful. They can also be quite entertaining—you never know what will float downstream next!

beaches can be just as satisfying as any other beach. Even though most rivers have currents, river beaches are still considered to be flat water because of their lack of surf.

Rivers offer unique challenges to swimmers, waders, paddlers, and powerboaters and can be very deceptive to all but the most seasoned river users.

Flooding

An ever-present possibility with most rivers is flooding. Temporary flooding can cause dangerously high and dirty water, strong currents, and dangerous debris both on and below the surface. Flooding can be experienced at riverfront beaches even during nice weather because heavy rains miles upstream and away from the beach can be the culprit. This is why it is vitally important for river beach managers to monitor regional weather patterns so they are not caught unaware. Dam openings upstream can also surprise swimmers. Unexpected flooding poses a threat to beachgoers; can sweep away buoys, lines, boats, and other beach equipment; and contributes to beach erosion. Another problem with rising rivers is that they actually seem to be calmer than rivers that are low and slow. This is because high waters often cover and disguise submerged objects so that rapids and white water, which usually indicate fast currents, are no longer obvious.

River Currents

The primary concern of the river beach is the perpetual current in the river. Unlike nearshore currents at great-water and ocean beaches that stop and start intermittently throughout the day and whose strength is associated with the height of the waves, river currents are ever present and relentless but perhaps not as noticeable. The intensity of river currents is not consistent across the width of the riverbed but rather fluctuates with the depth and contours in the river channel. Generally speaking, river currents travel more slowly near the riverbanks and faster on the surface and in the middle of the river. This can trick a swimmer or wader into thinking that because the river is calm at its banks, it is calm consistently across the river.

A significant hazard arises when swimmers attempt to cross smaller rivers and streams. Swimmers engaged in river crossings often find the river current to be much stronger than anticipated, and as a result, they end up downriver

much farther and quicker than anticipated. Then the troubled swimmers often mistakenly attempt to swim upriver against the current, which causes them to fatigue. This often results in panic and is one reason so many people drown while attempting to swim across even the smallest of rivers and streams. Often, those attempting to swim across rivers for the challenge are either intoxicated or wearing street clothes that weigh them down excessively when wet, adding to the problem. It is imperative to find the calmest water in a river to place a beach. Keeping boaters and motorized personal watercraft away from the swimming area is also extremely important.

Flotsam

Flotsam is large debris such as railroad ties, tree limbs, household appliances, and tires that is sent downstream either unintentionally or on purpose. Staying away from large floating objects is important, but even more important, swimmers should not get in front of these objects. When swimmers do get in front of flotsam, they can be submerged and trapped underneath or pinned against rocks, piers, pilings, or other immovable objects. Flotsam can also be moving underneath the surface of the river, causing the same problems for swimmers and waders along with the element of surprise that can lead to panic.

Low-Head Dams

Perhaps the greatest dangers in rivers and streams are created by low-head dams (small human-made structures). Low-head dams are life-threatening hazards found in many rivers and streams, and the eddies or hydraulics produced by waterfalls and dams can be catastrophic to those caught in them. The problem with low-head dams is that when unsuspecting swimmers or boaters mistakenly go over the falls because of a failure to recognize them, the circular water current, or treadmill, keeps the people just below the dam and actually pulls them underwater. This is because the waterfall produced by the water reentering the river immediately below the dam creates a strong downward and circular current. Because the hydraulic is aerated by falling water from above, victims are significantly less buoyant in the boil. Once caught in hydraulics or "drowning machines," victims are extremely difficult to rescue. Tragically, many rescuers have drowned in hydraulics while attempting to save others.

Do not get caught in the hydraulics of a low-head dam, such as this one on a stream in western Pennsylvania. Rescues are extremely difficult and often impossible.

Land-Based Beach Hazards

The risks posed by the water are not the only hazards at beaches. The beach material and other features of the land areas surrounding the water access can be dangerous.

Sand Entrapment

Digging holes and tunnels in the sand is very dangerous. Holes in the sand can cause trips and falls resulting in broken bones, and they can even be deadly. Because sand is so unstable, larger holes can collapse on people playing in the hole or tunnel. Beachgoers have been buried alive when holes and tunnels unexpectedly collapsed on them. Suffocation under the weight of the sand is the usual cause of death. Covering people in sand up to their necks has also led to serious injuries (e.g., beach vehicles can run over the person buried in the sand). Digging in the sand should not be allowed, and when it does occur, it should be stopped and the holes filled in immediately. Those digging in the sand should be advised as to why this is a dangerous practice.

Hot Coals

Burying hot coals is another dangerous practice because most visitors to the beach go barefoot. Coals can remain hot in the sand for hours and can cause serious burns to adults and especially small children. The younger the child stepping on hot coals, the more serious the injury can be.

Moving Vehicles

Any type of moving vehicle on the beach can present danger to unknowing patrons who are lying in its path. Common vehicles on the beach include those used for cleaning, rescue, or personal use if public driving is allowed on the beach.

Summary

All beaches are different. With those differences come challenges as well as risks and hazards. Highlighting the positive aspects of the beach while educating about, warning of, and supervising the risks and hazards is essential in making beaches safer and more enjoyable. Minimizing risks rather than eliminating risks should be the goal of the beach manager.

2

Beach and Waterfront Funding

Andrew Mowen
Pennsylvania State University

Although we have had beaches on our shorelines since the beginning of time, obtaining, maintaining, and safeguarding beach access come at a cost. This chapter explores how cost issues can be addressed. Balancing cost–benefit ratios is important when exploring funding options. Finding funding may transform a good beach into a great beach.

High-quality

High-quality beaches and waterfronts have significant environmental, social, and economic benefits. Beaches can provide community-wide benefits such as increasing tourism, public revenues, and real estate markets. These settings can also provide individual benefits through enhanced recreation experiences and through preservation of personal property. The extent to which beaches are able to meet these public and private needs relies heavily on the availability of fiscal resources. Like many other recreation areas, beaches require significant ongoing financial support for renourishment projects (e.g., beach restoration), improving public access, maintaining beach quality (e.g., litter removal), and ongoing beach operations (e.g., lifeguards, special events). Historically, public financing of park and recreation facilities was almost exclusively funded through public dollars using tax levies and bond referendums. However, the tax revolt of the mid-1970s necessitated that park facility financing include a wider variety of funding options for both capital and operational needs (Crompton 1999). Today's funding mechanisms still include public financing through tax support but also include special assessments, grant support, corporate sponsorship, user fees, and trust funds.

Park and recreation professionals should understand the funds and financing that are available for beaches as well as how to acquire and administer those funding resources. It is imperative for beach and waterfront managers to diversify their financing with a combination of federal, state, and local funding sources and revenue streams. This chapter introduces core beach operations and capital needs that require fiscal resources and discusses the primary funding sources that can be used to finance beaches and waterfronts. Key principles that promote balancing beach expenditures across multiple constituencies are discussed.

Beach Funding Priorities

Multiple stakeholders contribute to beach expense needs. Successful beach funding strategies must consider a number of different stakeholders who live near these resources or who visit as part of their vacations. Failed beach funding initiatives are often a result of an imbalance between what constituents pay toward beaches and how much they benefit from these resources (Ravella 2008).

Beachfront property owners and businesses recognize the value of beaches to the livability of their local community and may desire beach costs to be pushed toward nonadjacent residents or out-of-town visitors. However, local residents who do not live adjacent to the beach may argue that beachfront property owners stand to benefit the most from beach projects and may desire to push costs toward the waterfront property owners (Ravella 2008).

Although everyone has a stake in healthy shorelines, some residents receive more economic, aesthetic, and utilitarian benefits than others. Given this inequality, successful funding strategies often balance the interests and costs (according to benefit formulas) for beachfront residents, other local residents, and out-of-town guests. Financing beach initiatives such as renourishment, access, and operations can be beneficial not only for the local area but also for state and federal priorities (e.g., coastal protection from weather-related events). Thus, state and federal funds should be used to offset local costs when possible. However, acquiring state and federal dollars can be difficult based on public perception that beaches are nonessential amenities benefitting a limited population. There are several beach expenditure categories including beach renourishment, maintenance, access, and programming. These specific expenditure categories will often dictate what type and combination of federal, state, and local funding sources are most applicable for a given beach or waterfront.

Beach Renourishment

Beaches are not a static resource and are subject to constraint erosion as well as periodic environmental threats (Douglass 2002). Although fortifying or renourishing eroding beaches is not without controversy, it can be an important strategy in sustaining property, recreation use, and ecosystem integrity. Beach renourishment involves placing additional sand onto eroding beaches in order to restore shoreline positions and increase the amount of sand available for beach activities. Renourishment can be expensive and may require a pooling of federal and state dollars to support local investment in beach renourishment projects. Renourishment costs can vary widely, with annual expenses ranging from $100,000 to $600,000 per mile (1.6 km) depending on the location and project complexity (National Oceanic and Atmospheric Administration n.d.). Funding policies for renourishment projects vary from location to location, but there has been a trend of creating continuous dedicated funding to support renourishment. Local governments tend to resist paying directly for beach renourishment projects without first considering state or federal support and the possibility of creating special assessments for constituents who stand to benefit economically from renourishment. Common renourishment activities include dune and berm enhancements, placement of coastal structures to support additional sand placement, and channel dredging.

Beach Maintenance

Beyond renourishment, beaches and beach structures also require regular and periodic main-tenance. Ongoing and preventive beach main-tenance can be assumed by local governments and by voluntary and nonprofit organizations that have a vested interest in the condition and safety of their beaches and waterfronts. In many instances, voluntary and service organizations choose to adopt a beach, agreeing to conduct periodic and routine maintenance tasks. These contributions result in significant personnel savings for beach and waterfront communities with limited maintenance staffing and budgets. For example, the city of Long Beach coordinates a highly successful 30-minute beach cleanup each month that attracts a wide range of organizations and people to volunteer in keeping the Belmont Shore clean and litter free.

Beach renourishment is a large and expensive undertaking. Because beaches add significantly to the quality of life while supporting the local economy, many expensive renourishment projects are often approved quickly.

Beach Access Enhancements

Depending on state and local laws, not all beach and waterfront property is freely accessible to the general public. As beach community populations grow, there is increased pressure to provide public access through outright land acquisition, fee-based memberships, and conservation and access easements. When acquiring access through means other than outright land purchases, shared-use partnerships and tax-break incentives are common. Beach access enhancement projects that do not involve fee-simple acquisition typically include provisions for establishing beach maintenance responsibilities and for providing landowner indemnification when access is made free to the public. Moreover, a number of private beaches do offer access opportunities to nonresidents at discounted rates using daily and seasonal passes. Such access fees can be controversial, particularly when there is ambiguity in defining public versus private ownership of shoreline. For example, in Greenwich, Connecticut, a number of beach nonresidents have opposed access fees on the basis of their discriminatory effects. Furthermore, efforts to formalize public beach access easements in Santa Barbara County, California, have involved controversy because landowners have sued to block efforts to formalize prior public landowner agreements connected to their properties.

Special Events and Programs

Visitor experiences at beaches are enhanced when local jurisdictions provide organized programming to facilitate recreation activities, educate the public about beach and waterfront resources, and increase community cohesiveness and attachment. Because beaches interface with water, they can facilitate a wide variety of land and water-based programs and events. Possible sporting activities include beach volleyball, competitive swims and triathlons, and sailing races. Music and food festivals can also occur on these resources. These types of programs require funding to ensure that adequate personnel, equipment, and support facilities are present to meet visitors' needs. Nonprofit organizations and governing bodies (usually local park and recreation departments) support these programs using operational funds generated through tax dollars, donations, event attendance fees, and corporate sponsorships. In some cases, revenues generated from

beach programs can be used to support beach restoration and maintenance needs.

For example, California's Mendocino Coast has hosted the World's Largest Salmon Barbeque festival since 1970, and the proceeds from this event are used to support salmon restoration programs in the county, including water pollution and in-stream flows (Salmon Restoration Association, n.d.).

Core Funding Sources

Potential funding sources for beaches and waterfronts are as varied as the number of expenditure needs. The type of beach or waterfront project (whether renourishment, access, or operations) usually dictates the most appropriate funding mechanism and the source selected. What follows is an overview of key beach funding and financing sources that are available, with specific examples of how communities have used and leveraged these resources.

Federal Grants and Appropriations

Although local funds support a majority of beach expenditures for ongoing operations and special projects, federal and state monies often augment these local sources through direct appropriations, grants, and cooperative agreements. Federal funds can provide significant support for beach renourishment and access, yet obtaining these dollars can be difficult for local jurisdictions, and eligibility for these grant dollars can be limited. Federal dollars are authorized through the Water Resources Development Act (WRDA), and these dollars typically account for 65 percent of total project costs, with the balance coming from state, local, and private sources (Ravella 2008). Appropriations stemming from this act can be allocated to the U.S. Army Corps of Engineers (USACE), the Federal Emergency Management Agency (FEMA), and the National Oceanic and Atmospheric Administration (NOAA). Funding is administered after a series of stages (reconnaissance, authorization and feasibility, appropriation and funding, and construction), which takes about five years to complete. The reality for most beach renourishment projects is that funding likelihood and time frames deter communities from seeking these federal funds, particularly for small-scale, single-community beach renourishment projects.

One example of federal funding appropriation involves the Coastal and Estuarine Land Conservation Program (CELCP), operated through NOAA's Coastal Services Center. This program is designed to protect coastal resources for ecological, recreational, historical, and aesthetic values and provides funds to states that have coastal and estuarine land conservation plans (Ocean and Coastal Resource Management n.d.). These states, in turn, nominate up to three significant beach or waterfront projects that meet this program's funding criteria. This program funds beach protection rather than beach acquisition projects. Moreover, CELCP funds may be augmented by other federal sources such as the Land and Water Conservation Fund (LWCF), provided that nonfederal funding (e.g., state, local, private) requirements are met. Proposed projects are considered by Congress for each fiscal year, and available funding levels depend on federal appropriations that year.

Another example of direct appropriations from federal sources includes those funds available to beaches and waterfronts in their efforts to recover from natural disasters. For example, North Carolina received a $4 million grant to finance ongoing repairs to improve beach access and use at Miramar Beach. Expenditures for this project were designated to repair damage incurred by Hurricane Dennis, and this grant was made available by FEMA under the Hazard Mitigation Grant Program (*Walton Sun* 2009). These grant dollars operated as a reimbursement for the county's expenditures including a reinforced parking facility, demolition projects, storm water management, and dune erosion control initiatives.

Federal appropriations through earmarks may also provide funding for beach and waterfront projects. For example, a special waterfront district in East Providence, Rhode Island, received

Workers clean the beaches by hand in Orange Beach, Alabama, to help rectify the incomprehensible damage done by the BP oil spill in 2010.

federal funds in the fiscal year 2009 from the Consolidated Appropriations Acts. This appropriation was directed to small businesses constructing or renovating beach or waterfront properties with green building design and other sustainable development approaches. Specific project expenditures included stormwater management and eradication of invasive grasses.

Finally, federal dollars available through transportation authorizations may also be used to support beach and waterfront improvements, particularly as they relate to shoreline boardwalks and bike lanes. For example, in 2002, the San Luis Obispo Council of Governments (SLOCOG) included a waterfront boardwalk project in their application for federal transportation enhancement funds. Beaches that offer significant opportunities for nonmotorized transit may consider federal transportation dollars as part of their financing for waterfront developments, particularly if they connect with other transportation priorities in the nearby community.

State Funding

In addition to federally funded initiatives (many of which pass through state governing bodies), the states themselves can allocate their own funds for local beach and waterfront projects. Some coastal states have a long-standing tradition and means of funding local and statewide beach projects. However, others have no dedicated funding mechanism and rely on federal and local dollars to support beach and waterfront initiatives.

For example, New Jersey established a non-lapsing Shore Protection Fund that is used to fund shoreline protection and maintenance (National Oceanic and Atmospheric Administration n.d.). The New Jersey state legislature approves funding based on a project priority ranking set by New Jersey's commissioner of the Environmental Protection Fund. However, the total funding amount available through this state program depends on the income derived from real estate transfer fees. In other words, its viability depends on the changing conditions of New Jersey's real estate market (e.g., new housing starts). A final mechanism used by New Jersey and other states is a coastal protection trust fund financed by fees from coastal protection license plate purchases. In New Jersey, this trust fund supports the state's adopt-a-shore program.

In another example, Florida's Bureau of Beaches and Coastal Systems uses the Beach

Erosion Control Program to provide 50 percent matching funds to county and municipal governments, community development districts, and other special taxing districts for shore protection and preservation. Approved beach projects under this long-standing program include renourishment activities, engineering and project design studies, sand transfer, and dune restoration and protection activities.

Finally, in North Carolina, state funding is available for enhancing beach access, transportation, and recreation support facilities (e.g., restrooms, fishing piers, parking lots). Here, the North Carolina Division of Coastal Management provides about $1 million annually in matching grants through its Public Beach and Coastal Waterfront Access Program to local governing bodies (North Carolina Department of Environment and Natural Resources 2008). These awards are intended to rehabilitate, improve, and increase pedestrian access to state beaches and waterfronts. Funding for this beach access program is housed in the North Carolina Parks and Recreation Trust Fund.

In summary, federal and state grants and appropriations can provide significant funding for a variety of beach and waterfront initiatives. However, the consistency of federal and state funding levels, specific funding requirements, and the competitive process to acquire these funds may lead local jurisdictions to consider alternative beach financing strategies that emphasize local funding sources such as taxation, user fees, and partnerships. Of these mechanisms, taxation is the most common.

Direct Taxation

Tax support from local sources can provide significant levels of support for beach and waterfront expenses. The type of beach expenditure needs dictate the fairness of taxing methods used. Black, Donnelley, and Settle (1990) suggest that taxes directed toward beachfront property owners for the purpose of renourishment are highly target effective because these people benefit the most from this kind of project. Taxing local constituents to provide beach access is less effective because local residents often require fewer support amenities (e.g., parking, accommodations) than do out-of-town guests. In some Florida communities, local property tax assessments can vary depending on the structures' distance to the beach. In other communities, however, overnight accommodation sales taxes target out-of-town visitors more effectively. Regardless of the type of tax used, local governments are advised to balance taxing schemes across local and nonlocal populations based on the benefits that are derived from the specific beach expenditures.

Property Taxes

Beachfront and beach town property tax assessments are a common source of funding for beach renourishment, operations, and maintenance expenditures. Property tax revenues are typically deposited into a local government's general fund, and allocations for beach-related costs are subject to annual budget negotiations at the county, municipal, or special district level. This type of tax support is heavily dependent on assessed real estate property values along waterfronts (and in nearby communities if the beach community is part of a special district). However, beach and waterfront tax rates and property assessments can pose significant challenges for smaller beachfront

businesses such as marinas and commercial fishing operations, particularly when assessments are based on the properties' highest and best use rather than its current use. Such formulas often increase assessment values to amounts that are more typical of taxes paid by beachfront condominiums and restaurants. Despite the ubiquity of property taxes, their role in financing beach and waterfront expenditures has diminished somewhat over the past two decades, and new forms of taxation and financial support have been created to fill beach funding gaps.

Accommodation or Occupancy Taxes

Out-of-town visitors who do not pay property taxes benefit from beach and waterfront improvements as much as, if not more than, local residents. Yet, beachfront residents and out-of-town visitors who use beachfront accommodations (e.g., hotels, rental homes, time-share properties, campgrounds) often avoid paying parking fees because of their close proximity to beach and

Hotel, motel, and resort beaches, such as these in San Juan, Puerto Rico, attract a significant tourist trade because of the perfect blend of sun, sand, and water. Many visitors prefer their lodging to be right on the water's edge.

waterfront resources. Thus, one mechanism for ensuring that these constituents contribute to beach expenses is through a renter's or overnight accommodation tax.

For example, Galveston, Texas, implemented a 3 percent hotel tax to provide tourist services including communications, lifeguarding, and beach cleaning (Gunter, Ditton, and Olson 1987). Once a hotel or bed tax has been established, competition for a portion of revenues can be significant and may pit a number of beach investments against one another. For example, the Tampa Bay Rays baseball organization targeted 1 percent of the 5 percent Pinellas County hotel tax to pay for a $450 million waterfront stadium (Sharockman and Van Sant 2008). However, this shift in hotel tax allocations could reduce the amount of money available to support annual beach renourishment projects across the county.

Sales Taxes

A generalized sales tax is another potential mechanism to fund beaches. Sales taxes typically apply across entire communities and are paid by local residents and out-of-town guests. Because of their nondiscriminatory properties, sales tax financing has less target effectiveness than do property tax and accommodation or occupancy tax schemes. Moreover, the amount of money available through this tax source is heavily dependent on economic conditions within the local community and the number of out-of-town guests who purchase goods during their beach visits. For example, the city of Ventura, California, has recently proposed a half-cent sales tax increase to offset state funding cuts. Approximately 15 percent of sales tax revenues from all purchases made in the city could be allocated for clean and safe beach projects designed to improve water quality.

Tax Increment Financing (TIF) Trust Funds

Trust funds can also be established for the express purpose of supporting beach rehabilitation and operations. These trusts can receive their funding from a variety of tax-related sources and may provide a more stable basis to finance beaches than annual appropriations from local governing bodies. For example, trust funds can be structured to receive dollars from annual tax increment financing (TIF). TIF is an increase in local (or special district) property taxes collected by a governing body over and above the amount collected in a base year. One attractive feature of this type of tax support structure is that dollars go into a fund that is perpetually dedicated to beach and waterfront projects.

Municipal Bonds

Beaches and waterfront development projects that do not involve operational or maintenance expenditures can also be financed through bond funding. Bond financing is a common mechanism for borrowing funds to pay for significant capital and acquisition expenditures at public park and recreation facilities (Crompton 1999). Bonds are low-interest loans approved by the electorate and made to local governing bodies for the purpose of financing significant capital expenditures. Repayment of these bonds is typically made over a 10- to 30-year period; thus, bond-financed beach projects should have long-term characteristics, effects, and benefits. For example, New Hanover County and the city of Wilmington, North Carolina, collaborated to pass a $35.5 million bond designed to enhance parks, green spaces, and cultural amenities. Approximately $1 million of this bond is designed to enhance waterfront access through new facility construction. Moreover, $600,000 from this bond was designated specifically for beach towns in New Hanover County. In addition, Beaufort County, South Carolina, passed a $40 million bond that would fund preservation of working waterfronts and included funding provisions for purchasing land.

User Access and Parking Fees

Fees are a targeted way to ensure that people who use recreation amenities pay to support their development, maintenance, and operations. Beaches and waterfronts can be partially financed by two fee types: user access fees and parking fees.

User access (or entrance) fees charge visitors for entering a beach or waterfront zone either on a daily per-visit basis or through a season pass. Beach communities in states with strong public trust doctrines may, however, find it difficult to institute access fees because of regulatory requirements, legal challenges, implementation costs, and concerns over reduced tourist visitation levels. Beyond a continuous access fee, it may be more reasonable to temporarily enact or increase existing beach user access fees in order to acquire funds for periodic and significant beach improvement projects. Several beach destinations in New Jersey charge user access fees through daily and seasonal passes.

Parking fees may also be used when facilities exist to support vehicles at beach and waterfront destinations. Although parking fees can generate revenue from day users who drive to the beach, they are less effective at targeting beach users who live or stay in hotels and motels within walking distance. Moreover, people may use beach or waterfront parking for means other than beach access (such as nearby restaurants, office space, and other nonbeach attractions).

The decision to use parking fees for beach expenditures often hinges on the amount of revenue that can be generated from existing and projected parking as well as whether this type of funding can be augmented with other sources to pay for ongoing beach operations and special projects. For example, Martin County, Florida, had considered charging boat trailer and beach parking fees through kiosks and parking meters in order to renovate existing boat ramps and pay for restroom cleaning and trash pickup near these areas. However, a survey of 28 Florida counties found that, of the 14 counties that collected fees for beaches and boat ramps, only 2 counties made money after accounting for implementation and collection costs (TCoast Talk 2009).

Nonprofit and Private Sector Partnerships

Partnerships, particularly those between nonprofit and for-profit groups, promote greater networking and potential for tapping into a variety of funding sources. While private sector groups may have access to greater sources of wealth, nonprofit groups may have a better sense of environmental and people concerns. Perhaps the best funding efforts may come from combining the work of for-profit and nonprofit groups.

Operational Partnerships

Funding beach operations such as maintenance, safety programs, and special events can be accomplished through resource-sharing partner-

ships. Partnerships are the voluntary pooling of resources (e.g., labor, information, capital) between two or more parties to achieve mutual, collaborative goals (Yoder and Ham 2005). Partnerships allow organizations to leverage existing staff, facilities, equipment, and funds to provide enhanced services and facilities. In many instances, partnerships allow beach and waterfront managers to provide services (e.g.,

Pier-to-pier swims in southern California are both popular and financially productive. These sponsored races attract hundreds if not thousands of participants.

routine maintenance, lifeguarding) without having to directly acquire funds through other mechanisms. Given that beaches provide a setting for recreation programs and special events, partnerships with local businesses (through corporate sponsorship agreements) may generate dollars and in-kind resources needed to offer programs and to pay for beach restoration activities.

For example, Salisbury Beach in Massachusetts offers an annual Sand & Sea Festival that is partially funded and supported by a wide variety of local businesses. Event sponsors include food and beverage, telecommunications, and financial service corporations. This beach festival provides opportunities for businesses to contribute and be recognized at different levels as presenting, gold, silver, or bronze sponsors.

Acquisition Partnerships

In addition to augmenting ongoing beach operations, interorganizational partnerships can be used to directly acquire beach property and access easements. Acquiring beach property can be an expensive proposition for local governing bodies and may require partnerships with intermediary organizations to make timely purchases of property before public support and funding are available. Nonprofit land trusts can offer bridge loads or can directly negotiate and purchase beach properties while local governing bodies seek project funding for fee-simple purchase from these intermediary owners. For example, in 2004, the Trust for Public Land (TPL) made an outright purchase of 200 feet (60 m) of beachfront property in Nassau County, Florida. TPL then partnered with Nassau County government to find the necessary public funds (e.g., $2.275 million from the Florida Communities Trust) so that the county could then purchase the land directly from TPL (Trust for Public Land 2005).

Summary

As a general principle, sustainable and stable beach funding requires a combination of approaches to distribute the costs across those who directly and indirectly benefit from beach projects. Indeed, blended funding schemes to support beach initiatives is becoming quite common. Typically these funding schemes include state funding support (via grants) augmented by matching local dollars from property taxes, hotel occupancy taxes, and user fees. Beach program and event expenditures are often covered through general budgets of local governing bodies, but it is becoming more common to support beach programs through partnerships, outright donations, and corporate sponsorship agreements. Regardless of the funding source, efforts should be made to balance the burden of payment on those constituents who benefit the most from the specific beach projects and programs. Beach and waterfront professionals should stay abreast of changes in federal and state grant programs and seek to establish dedicated local funding dollars to match these grants and appropriations. Given the popularity and changing conditions of our beaches, community leaders will need to understand and acquire a wide variety of beach funds in the coming years.

Accessibility

3

The mission of most beaches is to attract people of all shapes, sizes, colors, and abilities to the shoreline. There is nothing like the combination of sand, sun, and water to attract a crowd to the beach. Beach enjoyment should be for everyone, not just select populations. The beach experience will be more memorable if access to the sand and water is easy and user friendly for all visitors. Although this design concept can be costly in some cases, it is a wonderful investment that is sure to improve both safety and enjoyment at the beach.

The purpose of this chapter is to encourage beach managers and administrators to provide improved accessibility for people with disabilities. Rather than simply meet the minimum requirements of the Americans with Disabilities Act (ADA), it is hoped that those designing, constructing, and operating beaches will do everything possible to create an environment that welcomes *all* patrons and provides equal opportunities for everyone coming to the beach.

Going Beyond the ADA

Most often, accessibility means compliance with legal standards that allow for approach, entrance, and use of facilities by persons with disabling conditions. But accessibility is better viewed as a dynamic rather than a static term, more like a continuum that moves progressively and consistently from many barriers to few or no barriers.

The ADA is a federal civil rights law, passed in 1990, that prohibits all discrimination on the basis of disability by local governments (city parks, recreation departments, park districts, school districts), counties, state governments, and businesses as well as nonprofit organizations. The ADA law went into effect in 1992, but the Department of Justice published revised regulations for Titles II and III of the Americans with Disabilities Act of 1990 in the Federal Register on September 15, 2010. These regulations adopted revised, enforceable accessibility standards called the 2010 ADA Standards for Accessible Design. On March 15, 2012, compliance with the 2010 standards will be required for new constructions and alterations. In the period between September 15, 2010, and March 12, 2012, covered entities may choose between the 1991 standards (without the elevator exemption for Title II facilities), the Uniform Federal Accessibility Standards (Title II facilities only), and the 2010 standards. The 2010 standards have important technical requirements not only for swimming pools but also for accessible routes for boat slips, launches, launching ramps, boating and fishing piers, and platforms. Beach managers may need to know this technical information. For information about the ADA, including the revised 2010 ADA regulations, please visit the department's website (www.ADA .gov); for answers to specific questions, call the

toll-free ADA information line at 800-514-0301 (voice) or 800-514-0383 (TTY).

When it comes to outdoor recreation and beach accessibility, the law remains a work in progress. The latest ADA requirements for outdoor areas, including beaches, are in the draft final guideline phase, and while technically not law, they are now being enforced by many agencies. Go to www .access-board.gov and click on "outdoor areas" for more information. For specific information about making boating and fishing piers and docks more accessible, go to www.ada.gov under the 2010 ADA Standards for Accessible Design.

There are very few exemptions to the ADA. Any person with a health condition or disorder that has a significant effect on one or more major life-functioning areas, such as learning, working, walking, recreating, speaking, hearing, and procreating, is considered to be a person with a disability under the ADA. This broad definition protects roughly 50 million Americans from discrimination on the basis of disability. It also includes people with cognitive impairments, mental health disorders, cardiac conditions, and HIV.

Little information is available on making outdoor recreation facilities compliant, and even less information is available about beach accessibility from an ADA perspective. As a result, it is important for beach managers and operators to network and share information on how they are overcoming obstacles to accessibility. Two major barriers to beach accessibility are (1) inadequate information for people with disabilities and (2) poor attitudes toward those with disabilities and toward making facilities more accessible.

The ADA is modeled after the Civil Rights Act of 1964. Congress intended that local governments do more than the private sector. There are five sections in the ADA:

Title I: employment. This section requires reasonable accommodation of otherwise qualified persons in any and all aspects of the employer–employee relationship. This includes recruitment, interview, hiring, merit increase awards, professional development, office, communication tools, and vehicle access advancement.

Title II: services. This section relates to more than 86,000 units of state and local government. It prohibits discrimination solely on the basis of disability and requires the provision of reasonable modifications that will enable a person with

With the help of a portable mat, people using wheelchairs can easily traverse the soft sand. Without the mat, the wheelchairs would be unable to reach the water's edge.

a disability to participate in all aspects of public parks and recreation, including beaches. It also requires municipalities and counties to make recreation services available in an inclusive setting (i.e., where people with and without disabilities can interact together). The law now requires anything designed or built after January 26, 1992, to comply with access requirements. Further, it requires governments to evaluate existing recreation sites and facilities for access.

Title III: private entities providing public access. This section simply states that private entities are not required to comply as readily and as completely as are government units.

Title IV: communications. Title IV requires every telephone company in every state to establish a third-party telephone relay system. During the 1990s, these allowed people who were deaf or hard of hearing to use a typewriter device affixed to a telephone to have a real-time conversation with a person who is not deaf or hard of hearing through a translator. Fortunately for us today, this is more readily accomplished through text messaging.

Title V: enforcement. Enforcement options for ADA violations are greater today than ever before. Violations of the ADA can lead to both compensatory damage and civil penalty costs. These fines can easily exceed $100,000.

Policy Issues

There are numerous policy requirements that promote access and inclusion. As stated previously, the United States Congress intended that state and local governments do more than private entities to promote access and inclusion.

Notice and Invitation

The ADA requires agencies to inform the public how their compliance with the ADA will affect services to the public. This notice should also send a strong message that potential beachgoers with disabilities are welcome. The notice and invitation should not only invite people with disabilities to the beach but also inform the public that the agency is cognizant of the ADA and is ADA compliant. Both messages need to be strongly stated. For example, a simple notice such as the following should suffice: "The City of St. Francis invites everyone to enjoy Golden Sands Beach, including people with disabilities."

Inclusion

The ADA defines the most integrated setting as the one in which people with and without disabilities interact together to the maximum extent possible. A person with a disability who, with or without a reasonable accommodation, can meet the requirements of the program or class in which they are enrolling must be admitted to the beach or program. The following conditions apply:

• Capacity: When a class or beach is full and thereby closed to additional people, a person with a disability cannot trump others to gain admission and overfill the class or beach. In this case, the person with the disability can legally be denied access.

• Charges: Whenever a fee is charged for admission or participation, any person who is unable or unwilling to pay can legally be denied access to the beach or program. In this case, the denial is about the financial inability to pay, not the disability.

• Conduct: Appropriate conduct must be exercised by all those attending the beach or participating in a program. Rules and regulations apply to all people for their own safety, whether or not they are nondisabled or disabled. People with disabilities can be expelled when they break the rules.

• Capability: Many programs have skill prerequisites and requirements. For instance, lifeguards are required to have good hearing in order to become certified. The courts have ruled

that candidates who are deaf may be denied lifeguarding certification because the training agencies have placed a hearing requirement in the program to ensure safety of guests and so that lifeguards can better assist in an emergency. Likewise, scuba diving certification programs have a swimming requirement. A person with a disability who does not swim would be denied access to the program because of lack of requisite skill, not because of the disability.

Reasonable Accommodation

A reasonable accommodation is any person, policy, or thing that helps someone with a disability meet the essential eligibility requirements for the class or program. For example, to enter a lifeguard class you need good hearing and eyesight. Swimmers who are blind would not be accepted into a lifeguarding class because they cannot meet the eyesight requirements. When and how to provide specific reasonable accommodations may be better determined by a certified therapeutic recreation specialist. Providing reasonable accommodations may include providing beach walkovers, adding extra staff for assistance, providing sign language interpreters, changing rules and policies when appropriate, and providing adaptive equipment such as beach wheelchairs.

Unfortunately, finding and enjoying a truly accessible beach remains a hit-or-miss proposition. Rather than simply ask "What does the ADA require me to do?" perhaps the best approach for beach managers is to do their best to create an environment that welcomes all guests to the beach and provides equal opportunities for everyone. Some barriers to accessibility at beaches include the soft sand that impedes progress to the water's edge. The beach sand can be made more accessible through a combination of beach matting that allows wheelchair access and specially designed beach wheelchairs with large inflatable tires. Four-wheel drive vehicles can also assist patrons with disabilities across the sand and to the water's edge. Stairways over dunes, piers, and observation decks should be replaced with properly sloped ramps. Once ramps are installed at beaches, it is imperative to keep them free of sand and vegetation, which can be a recurrent problem. For flat-water beaches, wheelchair ramps can be installed directly into the water for excellent access.

Therapeutic recreation is often thought of as a swimming pool activity, but with the right equipment, therapeutic recreation can be easily and successfully adapted to the open water.

To make any particular beach more accessible, the best resources may be found locally. Support groups in the local community can provide up-to-date and specialized information on specific disabilities. Often these groups are happy to speak to beach staff and lifeguards before the summer or during in-service training. Some of these groups include but are not limited to the following:

- Deaf Center
- Disabled American Veterans
- Lions Eye Bank
- National Multiple Sclerosis Society
- Muscular Dystrophy Association
- United Cerebral Palsy

Again, refer to the updated 2010 standards for boating and fishing docks and piers, available online at www.ada.gov under the 2010 ADA Standards for Accessible Design.

Attitudes

Being ADA accessible means so much more than providing physical access to the beach and its related facilities. In addition to physical accessibility, it is important to provide a welcoming environment through appropriate communications.

Staff training that promotes positive attitudes toward people with disabilities is of paramount importance. Enhancing communication skills, eliminating stereotypes, creating empathy, and strengthening positive attitudes should all be integral parts of training. Many staff members do not consider themselves biased, bigoted, or insensitive, but patronizing tones or statements, insensitivity, and an unwelcoming attitude can create significant barriers to those with disabilities. Like most everything else, communication is the key. There is no need to bring up a disability in conversation. Asking a person with a disability how he is "holding up" may be irritating or embarrassing. Likewise, making hurried, last-minute changes to make a beach or facility more accessible may only bring unwanted attention to someone with a disability. Choosing the wrong words can be particularly damaging. Although many people attempt to be politically correct, the terms *disabled* and *handicapped* are no longer appropriate in most situations. Referring to people as deaf, blind, spastic, or epileptic is not necessary and may be thought unkind. People with disabilities like to be as independent as possible and should always be asked if they need assistance; staff should never assume they need help. When speaking to someone in a wheelchair, it is always a good idea to kneel down to achieve good eye contact rather than look down while speaking. Staff should not feed or pet working assistance animals. These are just a few suggestions to improve communication and attitude.

Guidelines From the Recreation Access Board

The latest accessibility guidelines for outdoor developed areas are still being finalized by the ADA. The final guidelines apply to all federal land management agencies but will also apply to private entities, state and local governments, and nonprofits that construct or alter outdoor and beach facilities on federal property or have an arrangement with a federal agency to do so. The new laws will mostly deal with access to the beach. More specifically, they concern beach access routes that connect to entry points for high tide level at tidal beaches; mean high water level at river beaches; and normal recreation water level at lake, pond, and reservoir beaches. Specific

requirements regarding clear widths, obstacles, openings, slopes, resting intervals, protruding objects, and elevated dune crossings are all addressed in the latest requirements, along with exceptions granted for the new rules. These are still being finalized. For further information, go to www.access-board.gov and click on "outdoor areas" or call 202-272-0080 or 202-272-0014.

Summary

Beaches can be among the most desirable recreation destinations, but for many people with disabilities, beaches can be enormously uninviting and even dangerous because of poor planning or poor attitudes. Few, if any, beaches are fully accessible to everyone, and certainly the soft sand produces one of the most challenging obstacles on the beach. Careful and creative long- and short-term planning can have a significant positive impact on beach accessibility. Likewise, positive attitudes by beach staff go a long way toward improving beach accessibility. Many references and resources are available on the Internet to assist you in making your beach more accessible. Finding support groups and local people with disabilities to speak to your beach staff before each season may be the best investment in making your beach more accessible and inviting to all.

Liability and Risk Management

Shawn DeRosa
Pennsylvania State University

For the pros, risk management is nothing more than structured, organized common sense. But for those who do not spend most of their time as risk managers, risk management can be a daunting task. The goal of risk management is to reduce hazards and risks, not eliminate them, and this chapter goes a long way in getting you to see and understand the big picture in risk management as it applies to beaches and ancillary features and functions. Developing a specific written risk management plan will help you visually detect hazards and risks with ease.

Water-based recreation is widely popular around the world. Like any sport, with all aquatic activities there comes a certain level of risk that participants come to expect. The risks in water-based recreation are similar to those of activities performed on land, including the potential for catastrophic head, neck, or back injuries. However, unlike many land-based activities, the risk of drowning is ever present whenever in, on, or around the water.

With the growing popularity of water-based recreation, it is reasonable to assume that beach managers will at some point be faced with an incident that may result in litigation. From simple slips and falls resulting in injury to deaths occurring in the water, beach owners, managers, and lifeguards may find themselves parties to a lawsuit either alleging negligent behavior or seeking recovery for injuries sustained while on the premises. This chapter explores both of these common causes of legal action and examines strategies to reduce the risk of injury and financial loss.

Negligence

Negligence occurs when someone, owing a duty of care to another, fails to act reasonably in fulfilling that duty, thereby causing harm. In essence, negligence is doing something that a reasonably prudent person in a similar situation would not have done (misfeasance) or, alternatively, failing to do that which a reasonably prudent person would have done (nonfeasance). In most cases, negligence is an unintentional act resulting from carelessness or inattention to one's duties. In other words, the defendant never intended for someone to become injured; it just happened. However, in some cases intentionally negligent acts (malfeasance) may result in liability, including criminal liability. For a party to be found negligent, the plaintiff must establish each of the four elements of a negligence claim: duty, breach of duty, causation, and damages.

Duty

A legal duty is an obligation, recognized by law, to conform to a certain standard of conduct designed to protect others against unreasonable risks of injury. A duty to act is said to arise out of a special relationship between the parties (e.g., parent and child, teacher and student, coach and athlete, lifeguard and swimmer, beach manager and patrons). A legal duty may also arise out of contract or in some cases by the voluntary assumption of a duty, such as when a Good Samaritan provides first aid when not otherwise required by law to do so. In the aquatic context, the duty of an aquatic director, lifeguard, or instructor is to take steps to protect participants from unreasonable risks of harm.

In determining whether a duty has been fulfilled, courts will ask whether the conduct in question met the standard of care in the industry. There are generally three classifications for the standard of care. The lowest standard is that of the reasonable person. (What would a reasonably prudent person do in the same situation?) Where a special relationship exists between the parties (e.g., parent and child), the law requires a slightly elevated standard. The highest standard of care is owed by professionals and thus has been named the professional standard.

In the United States, no duty of care exists between strangers. Should a beach patron notice someone caught in a rip current, the law does not require that patron to initiate a rescue. There is in fact no legal duty to rescue strangers. However, if a patron chooses to initiate a rescue, the standard then shifts, and the patron is said to have voluntarily assumed a duty of care. The patron's rescue attempts would be evaluated according to the reasonable person standard. If later sued, courts will look to see whether the patron's conduct reflects that which other reasonably prudent patrons in similar situations would have done, including continuing care until properly relieved by emergency medical personnel. If the patron stopped rendering care before the arrival of emergency medical crews or without being relieved by someone of equal or superior training, the patron might be successfully sued for abandonment.

Parents possess a special relationship with their children. If a mother sees her child caught in a rip current, the mother is deemed to have an elevated duty of care. She cannot simply walk away while allowing her child to be swept to sea. Instead, she must act reasonably to help her child in accordance with her own ability level. This may mean initiating a rescue attempt if able to do so or, at a minimum, summoning additional help. If the parent is a nonswimmer, the law would not require the parent to endanger her own life by attempting a rescue but would expect the parent to do something other than stand by idly while her child struggled in the water.

Rescuing a swimmer from a rip current is extremely risky and often impossible. Here, a scuba diver is being rescued from the grip of a large rip.

By contrast, lifeguards on a beach have the highest standard of care. They are expected to act as other reasonably prudent professional rescuers (lifeguards) would act under similar circumstances. During litigation, expert witnesses will testify as to what the applicable professional standards are in any given situation. These experts will look to state laws and local regulations to help determine what standards apply in a given jurisdiction. Further, position statements and manuals from professional groups and training organizations may also help form the standard of care. Although the United States Lifesaving Association (USLA) does not own or operate beaches, the organization does publish an authoritative manual for open-water lifesaving and provides certification to beaches that meet certain training standards. The guidelines, recommendations, and training standards espoused in the USLA manual would likely be used to help define the standard of care as applied to open-water lifeguards even if the beach where the injury occurred was not affiliated with the United States Lifesaving Association.

Breach of Duty

A breach of duty occurs when the responsible party fails to uphold the applicable standard of care. When a beach manager fails to properly supervise staff (e.g., by failing to provide training or failing to provide adequate on-site supervision), this would constitute a breach of the duty to supervise. Failing to provide warning signs calling attention to dangerous conditions on the premises could be considered a breach of the duty to provide reasonably safe facilities. Failing to properly inspect and maintain play structures and equipment could be a breach of the duty to provide safe equipment.

Causation

Once a plaintiff establishes that the defendant breached a duty of care, the plaintiff must then introduce evidence to show that the breach itself caused the plaintiff's injuries. There must be a direct causal relationship between the breach and the harm suffered. (Was the defendant's negligence the actual cause of the plaintiff's injuries?) The more distant the breach is from the injury, the less likely it is that the defendant will be found negligent. If the injury would have occurred without any act or failure to act on the part of the defendant, then there is no causal connection, and the defendant will not be found negligent. Courts will also consider whether the harm suffered by the plaintiff was the reasonably foreseeable result of the defendant's actions. The law requires only that beach managers take steps to protect patrons from reasonably foreseeable injuries. A look back at prior incident reports, first aid reports, and even newspaper articles will give the new beach manager an idea as to what types of accidents and injuries are likely to occur at any given beach.

Harm or Damages

Essential to any claim for negligence is the element of damages or harm. Damages, commonly defined, include physical, financial, or emotional injuries suffered by the plaintiff. In the aquatics environment, physical harm may be in the form of deep lacerations; broken bones; complications from a submersion incident; head, neck, or back injuries; or drowning. Plaintiffs expect to be compensated for these injuries and for any pain and suffering they may have experienced. Compensatory damages are intended to compensate a person for harm suffered. Lost wages, medical expenses, and restitution for damages to property are common examples of compensatory damages.

Because most recreation activities involve some degree of contact (either with equipment, a playing surface, or another participant), minor scrapes and bruises generally are not considered significant enough to warrant legal action. These minor injuries are often considered inherent in the activity, and thus liability would not attach. In some states, emotional harm such as loss of companionship is also actionable. Punitive damages are generally an extra award of money designed to punish the wrongdoer and to discourage the same harmful behavior in the future. Punitive damages are generally reserved for extreme cases where the defendant's behavior is so outrageous that it shocks the conscience of the court.

Negligence Per Se

In some situations, the concept of negligence per se may hold a defendant liable for damages resulting from the violation of a safety regulation or law, provided that the plaintiff is within the class of persons the law was designed to protect. Federal law, for example, requires coastal beach operators to close their beaches whenever bacteria levels exceed a given threshold. Assume that a beach manager chose to remain open despite the known presence of bacteria levels exceeding state

and federal limits. Assume, further, that dozens of people then became ill with a gastrointestinal illness as a result of swimming at the beach. Because the decision to stay open violated the safety statute that mandated closure, and because the people who got sick were in the class of people the law was designed to protect (beachgoers), the beach manager could be found negligent per se.

Degrees of Negligence

Contrary to popular belief, merely establishing that a defendant was negligent may not alone result in judgment in favor of the plaintiff. Depending on state laws, some public recreation providers may be immune from negligence suits unless the plaintiff can establish some degree of negligence beyond ordinary negligence. Under the ordinary negligence standard, a defendant is responsible for using reasonable (ordinary) care to protect the plaintiff from reasonably foreseeable injuries. Examples of ordinary negligence include failure to properly supervise staff and failure to inspect rescue equipment.

In some instances, the law may require a plaintiff to prove gross negligence in order to be successful against a public entity or in order to allow for punitive damages. Gross negligence is conduct that goes beyond accidental oversight or mistake. Gross negligence is akin to intentional failure to fulfill one's legal obligations, with disregard for the consequences. It can be described as unreasonable conduct that is known, or should reasonably be known, to have the potential for injury. Examples of gross negligence include failure to provide adequate safety equipment despite the presence of known dangers and failure to inspect a beach for underwater hazards that are known to develop over time.

Conduct that is so unreasonable that it is said to be in flagrant disregard of safety standards, thereby endangering life and limb, is termed willful, reckless, or wanton misconduct.

Defending Negligence Claims

Although in the United States the burden is on the plaintiff to establish each of the elements of his negligence claim, there are certain defenses that will either reduce or eliminate liability on the part of the defendant. Preparing for negligence claims in advance should be an integral part of any risk management program. Employing strategies such as issuing group use permits is an important step in defining expectations of beach users, particularly large groups that come to the beach with dozens of children but with minimal adult supervision. Waiver forms are also an important step in defusing negligence liability, particularly as related to the use of specialty equipment (e.g., in-water trampolines, canoes, banana boats) or special programs (e.g., scuba).

In the sport context, many jurisdictions (although not all) allow the defendant to claim that the plaintiff assumed the risk of injury by participating in the sport. To succeed under the assumption of risk doctrine, the defendant must show that the plaintiff not only understood the risks inherent in the sport but also voluntarily agreed to assume those risks. This can be a difficult task in the aquatic environment because many beachgoers do not fully appreciate the risks of rip currents or the dangers of crashing waves. Warning signs and educational material may help put beachgoers on notice of the dangers associated with a given beach. The prudent beach manager would take reasonable steps to educate patrons about the known dangers on the beach despite the fact that the law may consider some of these dangers obvious (thus making a warning sign unnecessary).

The law expects recreation participants to use due care around the water. What is reasonable in any given situation may depend on the knowledge and skill of the person involved. A person with years of boating experience would be held to a higher standard than would a novice boater.

Contributory and Comparative Negligence

When the conduct of the plaintiff fails to meet the standard of self-protection expected of persons with similar skill and experience, then the plaintiff may be found to have contributed to her own injury (contributory negligence). If the plaintiff's own actions played a significant role in causing her own injuries, the defendant will not be liable even though the defendant's actions or failure to act may also have played a role in causing the injury. In essence, in the few states that still follow the doctrine of contributory negligence,

any contributory negligence on the part of the plaintiff will be a complete bar to recovery.

Most states have adopted a form of comparative negligence wherein the plaintiff's recovery will be reduced by his own percentage of fault. In such pure comparative jurisdictions, even if a plaintiff is 75 percent responsible for his own injury, he would nevertheless recover a judgment for his injuries, reduced then by his degree of fault. For example, if the plaintiff's total award was for $100,000, the judge would reduce the amount to be recovered by 75 percent, thus reducing the recovery to $25,000.

Beach volleyball tournaments are overwhelmingly popular. Organized events such as these should require participants to sign a statement of understanding as well as a waiver.

Some states follow a somewhat different approach to comparative negligence wherein the plaintiff cannot recover anything if the plaintiff contributed equally to his injuries or, in some states, if the plaintiff was more at fault than the defendant.

Governmental Immunity

Historically, under the doctrine of sovereign immunity, the government could not be sued without its consent. This resulted in a somewhat unfair result when a person was injured or killed as a result of her use of government-owned or -operated programs and facilities. All states have now enacted tort reform allowing government agencies to be sued under certain circumstances, such as the negligent operation of public facilities. The right to sue the government is not absolute, however. Policy decisions and decisions related to the allocation of public resources, for example, cannot be the subject of a lawsuit. As such, the decision whether to provide lifeguard services at a city-owned or -operated swimming beach is often protected as a discretionary function and is thus immune from suit. However, should a government agency decide to provide lifeguard services at a public beach and then fail to operate the beach in accordance with applicable standards of care in the industry, resulting in harm, a lawsuit would be allowed.

Good Samaritan Statutes

All states have enacted laws to encourage bystanders to render emergency care to injured persons. These Good Samaritan statutes provide immunity from claims of ordinary negligence. Although laws vary from state to state, all Good Samaritan laws are based on public policy: It is in our collective best interest to encourage persons to render care to another in time of need without the fear of a lawsuit acting as a barrier to becoming involved. Good Samaritan statutes provide immunity from civil suit to those persons who *voluntarily* and *in good faith* render care at the scene of an emergency. Those persons who voluntarily assume care of an injured person owe a duty of reasonable care to the injured party. Because most Good Samaritan statutes provide protection from claims of ordinary negligence, if a plaintiff establishes that the caregiver's actions were grossly inappropriate and contributed to the plaintiff's injuries, the Good Samaritan protections may not apply. However, the burden of proving gross negligence is high, and concerns about gross negligence should not stop someone from rendering care.

Persons who are paid to provide care or medical assistance, such as on-duty police officers, firefighters, emergency medical technicians, and lifeguards, are not said to be acting voluntarily but rather out of an employment obligation. Similarly, because persons who expect to be compensated for rendering assistance are not deemed to be acting voluntarily, the Good Samaritan statutes would not apply. Some states have enacted separate laws to limit liability of on-duty rescue workers. It is therefore beneficial to contact a legal professional to review the laws of the state in which you work or reside.

Premises Liability

Another area of law that beach managers should be familiar with is premises liability. The duty of care owed to beach visitors may vary depending on the character and intended use of the property. Under the theory of premises liability, landowners are liable for injuries sustained by land entrants in varying degrees based on the status of the land entrant and the status of the property itself. Where the property remains in its natural condition, with no alterations, little, if any, liability would attach. Liability begins to arise once you alter the natural condition of the property, such as by grooming the beach, installing sanitary facilities and picnic areas, or clearing weeds or replenishing sand. Where human-made alterations exist, the landowner's duty of care will often depend on the status of the land entrant. Persons who enter another's property are generally classified as trespassers, licensees, or business invitees.

Trespassers

Trespassers are those who enter land without the knowledge or permission of the landowner. Although many landowners would argue that they should have no legal duty to protect trespassers on their land, the law is somewhat different. Landowners owe a minimal level of care—they must avoid intentionally or recklessly injuring trespassers. Beyond this minimal duty to avoid intentionally or recklessly causing injury, landowners have no duty to inspect their premises, provide warnings, or make their properties safe for trespassers. However, where a landowner has knowledge of trespassers, the landowner then owes a duty of reasonable care to warn of dangerous conditions, including ongoing projects. Of note, where children of tender years (often defined as six years of age and under) trespass onto a landowner's property, the landowner may be deemed to have a slightly elevated duty of care when a condition of or on the property may be construed as an attractive nuisance. Where the property is found to attract children, landowners must take reasonable steps to restrict access to dangerous areas so as to prevent injury to young children.

Licensee

Where a landowner gives permission for a land entrant to be present on the property and where such land entrant is present for his own personal interest or gain, such individual is said to be a licensee. For example, at beaches where no admission fee is charged, beachgoers would be considered licensees. They are at the beach for their own personal reasons, whether it be to swim in the water or relax on the sand. Social guests would be licensees; they bring no economic benefit to the landowner. In these situations, landowners owe a duty of reasonable care to protect licensees from known hazardous conditions. The landowner must repair dangerous conditions on the premises or, alternatively, provide warnings of those conditions that cannot be repaired. Warnings related to underwater obstructions, sudden drop-offs, steep slopes, and dangerous currents are well advised to demonstrate reasonable steps taken to provide notice of known dangerous conditions.

Invitees

Land entrants who are present for the benefit of the landowner (e.g., when a fee is charged) are said to be invitees. Where the landowner stands to benefit from use of her property, the law imposes a slightly elevated duty of ordinary care. The landowner must not only take reasonable steps to protect invitees of known dangerous conditions on the premises but also protect against those dangers of which she should reasonably be aware. In other words, landowners owe a duty to invitees to inspect the premises for danger-

ous conditions, remove or repair those that are found, and provide cautionary warnings of those dangers that cannot be removed or repaired. A prudent risk management strategy would be to require and to document routine inspections of the premises as one method of establishing a reasonable approach to managing the property.

Recreational Use Statutes

States have enacted recreational use statutes to limit private landowners' responsibility for injuries to persons who use their land for recreation. These statutes have been interpreted to also include liability protection for public landowners, including municipalities and state governments. The purpose of these statutes is to encourage private landowners to allow the public onto private land for recreational purposes without the fear of being responsible for injury. Important to note is that each state's statute may differ in the level of protection offered.

Integral in many recreational use statutes, such as the Massachusetts statute (21 Mass. Gen. Laws 17C), is the requirement that the landowners not charge for the land use. In states that impose a no-fee requirement, charging an admission fee may remove any sort of recreational use statute protection. Fees for parking, however, have been permitted. Other states set a limit on the maximum amount of money a landowner may collect annually before losing the protection of the statute. For example, the Wisconsin Recreational Use Statute (Chapter 895.52) not only offers protection against attacks by wild animals but also allows property owners to collect up to $2,000 annually from persons using the property for recreational use before statutory protections are lost. In all cases, these types of statutes will not protect against willful, wanton, or reckless conduct by landowners, including the failure to warn against known hazardous conditions on the property.

Risk Management

Risk management is an ongoing process of identifying, evaluating, and controlling risk of injury or financial loss through a systematic analysis of all aspects of your aquatic program. Although many texts offer detailed risk management plans, people operating swimming beaches need practical advice on how to address those risks common in the industry. The risk management process proposed involves the following:

1. Identifying risks
2. Eliminating risks whenever possible
3. Evaluating the likeliness and frequency of occurrence in addition to the potential severity of the risk
4. Selecting steps to minimize the risk
5. Documenting the process
6. Using insurance and other risk allocation devices, specifically waivers and releases

Risk Identification

Waterfront managers should inspect the premises routinely and identify conditions that could result in physical injury or financial loss. Additionally, managers should make note of any dangerous practices of staff that could result in injury (e.g., failure to use personal protective equipment) as well as potential risky behaviors of patrons (e.g., headfirst entries into shallow water). Policies and procedures should be reviewed to ensure they are consistent with state, federal, and local laws and regulations. Facilities and equipment should be inventoried, valued in case of future loss (e.g., theft, vandalism, fire), and inspected for deterioration or needed repairs.

At this stage of the risk management process, managers should perform a risk audit, creating a list of potential risks, including those obvious to patrons (e.g., risk of falling over the edge of a cliff) and those that are not so obvious (e.g., the dangers of rip currents). As part of the risk identification process, managers should become familiar with local, state, and federal laws and regulations that relate to activities at the waterfront area. Copies of relevant health codes, state statutes, and the like should be kept on file and shared with the management team. Similarly, managers should examine all policies and procedures to ensure they are in writing and available to employees, often listed in an employee handbook. Policies with respect to appropriate behavior, appearance, attendance, and the use of alcohol and drugs before or during work should be periodically reviewed to ensure they are consistent with relevant laws and judicial decisions.

When inspecting the premises for potentially dangerous conditions, it is important to consider both obvious and hidden dangers. Patrons owe themselves a duty to use reasonable care to protect themselves against self-injury. Dangers that are readily apparent to the average person ought to be easily avoided. As such, there is generally no duty to provide warnings of those dangers that are considered open and obvious. However, where there is a duty to protect patrons from reasonably foreseeable harm, providing warnings of known dangers even if obvious would help demonstrate a reasonable approach to managing a facility.

As managers look to identify dangerous staff practices, consider issues such as physical altercations with guests and the possibility of staff choosing not to wear assigned personal protective equipment such as gloves, eye protection, and face masks. Similarly, identifying dangerous behaviors of patrons is an important step in developing reasonable rules and regulations for the beach area. Do parents stay within arm's reach of children? Can patrons identify rip currents? Do patrons use inflatable rafts or arm floats in place of lifejackets approved by the United States Coast Guard? The simple approach to risk identification is to always ask, "What if?" What if someone were to enter the water headfirst? What if a parent falls asleep while his young child is at the beach? By asking "what if?" you should identify common areas of risk in preparation for the next step in your overall risk management plan.

Risk Elimination

It may sound simple, but if a risk can be eliminated without ruining the activity, then perhaps it should be eliminated. If broken glass is present, it should be quickly and carefully removed to prevent lacerations. Defective equipment should be taken out of service and then repaired or replaced. However, in the recreation setting, particularly in an open-water environment, many risks cannot be eliminated. This is when a careful evaluation of the risk is needed to determine how to best manage the danger while minimizing the risk of injury or financial loss.

Risk Evaluation

All risks must be evaluated as to frequency of occurrence and severity of outcome. Managers are most concerned about risks that result in moderate to severe outcomes, including the potential for catastrophic injury or death. These risks require substantial oversight and management as part of the risk-reduction strategy. Similarly, risks that may result in less severe injury or financial loss but that occur frequently may also require substantial management. Small but frequent payouts and settlements over time add up to significantly larger amounts. Once each risk is evaluated as to its likelihood of occurrence and the severity or outcome should it occur, managers should then consider what level of management is needed to reduce the likelihood of occurrence.

Risk Minimization

In the aquatic arena, many risks cannot be eliminated. The risk of drowning is ever present whenever in, on, or around the water. Although the frequency of a drowning event is low, the severity is high, thus requiring substantial management of the risk. What can be done to minimize the risk of drowning? Should lifeguard services be offered? Should you require lifejackets for all nonswimmers, and if so, do you provide them free of charge? Do you have a group use policy for special user groups, requesting assistance of group supervisors in monitoring the behaviors of group members? Should a shallow-water play area be defined with ropes and buoys to help prevent young children from going too deep into the water? Do you have check-in and checkout procedures for boating equipment, and do you require watercraft users to put on lifejackets before boarding the craft? Do you advise against headfirst entries or post warning signs or flags for hazardous conditions such as rip currents?

Options to manage each risk should be carefully considered. Beach managers would be well advised to consult with owners and operators of similar facilities to learn how others manage the types of risks identified. Action steps should be identified for each risk, explaining the level of management needed and the specific steps to be taken to help reduce the frequency of occurrence.

Documentation

Documentation is an important step in the risk management process. Often we hear, "If it wasn't documented, it wasn't done." This is a good rule to follow. From a defense perspective, it is helpful to demonstrate through documentation all the preventive steps taken to reduce the risk of injury. Opening and closing checklists, incident reports, injury reports, prehire selection and evaluation procedures, in-service training and performance audit records, and other similar documents are useful to demonstrate to a jury that reasonable steps were taken to properly manage a given water area. Although many defense attorneys caution against documenting too much, a lack of routine documentation often creates the appearance of impropriety. Further, from a warranty perspective, many products require routine inspection and maintenance. For warranty service, it is often incumbent upon the owner to provide documentation that the product has been maintained according to the manufacturer's recommendations. Failure to provide evidence of required maintenance may nullify a warranty.

Risk Transfer

Transferring risk involves shifting the risk to another party. Common examples of risk transfer include insurance, waiver forms, release forms, assumption of risk forms, and agreements to participate.

Insurance

Many recreation providers could not afford to pay a large verdict or settlement without risking going out of business. Insurance is used as a way to transfer the financial risk to a third party, the insurance company, or a risk pool. For most small recreation providers, an insurance policy with a minimum of US$1 million coverage is sufficient to provide for most lawsuits. However, in the case of catastrophic injury or death, US$1 million may not be enough to fulfill a verdict. Consult your insurance agent to determine the extent of coverage needed for the activities occurring at your facility.

Waiver of Liability

Waivers are an essential element of a risk management plan. A waiver, signed before participation, is essentially a contract in which the participant agrees to waive, or relinquish, the right to sue for injuries that may result from ordinary negligence. Although the law regarding the validity of waivers varies from state to state, many states will uphold a properly worded waiver against adult participants. This requires that waivers be carefully worded to be clear and unambiguous and to include appropriate terminology as may be required in the state in which the activity occurs. Waivers should be written or reviewed by legal counsel. Some states (a minority of jurisdictions) also uphold waivers signed on behalf of a child under the age of 18 years, while the majority of states do not allow parents to give up their child's right to sue for injury. Other states disallow waivers completely, holding that they violate public policy. Regardless of their validity, waivers come strongly recommended because they may discourage a lawsuit from ever being filed. If a waiver is found by a court to be invalid, the organization is no worse off than had no waiver been used in the first place.

Release of Liability

Similar to a waiver, a release of liability seeks to protect an organization from legal action. A release is a contract in which one party relinquishes existing claims against another, often in exchange for some sort of settlement. In common usage, the terms *release* and *waiver* have come to be used almost interchangeably, despite the subtle legal distinctions between the two.

Assumption of Risk and Agreement to Participate

Some, but not all, states allow a defense theory of assumption of risk. This legal doctrine states that a participant voluntarily assumed the risk of injury inherent in any given activity in deciding to participate. Many organizations utilize an assumption of risk form as part of their risk management plan. The defense of assumption of risk is based on communicating to participants those risks of injury that are reasonably foreseeable. Although this is often done in the assumption of risk form itself, many recreation providers now use agreements to participate as a means of putting participants on notice of the potential for injury.

Managing Aquatic Facilities

Managers of aquatic facilities, including public swimming areas, must be familiar with a variety of legal issues surrounding employment relationships, including employment of minors, contract law, and of course civil rights law.

Employment Relationships

Employment relationships consist of regular employees (either at will or contracted) and independent contractors. It should be noted that independent contractors are not employees per se, but they can be deemed employees subject to the level of direction and control the employer asserts over their work.

Regular Employees

Most employees are considered regular; that is, the employer, often in exchange for payment of wages or salary, has the right to supervise and control the employees' daily work duties and assignments. Volunteers also fall into the category of regular employees, despite the fact they do not receive compensation. The employer is obligated to provide a nondiscriminatory work environment, safe working conditions, and the resources and supplies needed by employees to perform the work. Under the doctrine of vicarious liability, employers are responsible for all actions within the scope of an employee's employment. Employers are not liable for actions that are not work related. Managers may also be personally liable for hiring incompetent employees or failing to perform a thorough background check of potential employees.

Most employees are also considered at will, meaning their employment may be terminated for any nondiscriminatory reason or for no reason at all. Employers who explain a progressive discipline process in their employment manuals would be well advised to follow the process of progressive discipline before terminating an employee.

Contracted employees are given a contract that explains the terms and dates of employment, rate of pay, and the reasons the agreement may be terminated before the end of the contracted term. Union employees, often working in specific bargaining units, are a form of contract employee. The terms of their employment are explained in a bargaining agreement (contract) that governs their employment. Although true contracted positions in aquatics are rare, in those cases where a contract does govern the terms of employment, managers should become familiar with the contract and follow its guidelines for disciplining employees.

Independent Contractors

Independent contractors, like contracted employees, have a contractual right to perform a job. These contractors are self-employed, meaning they are not employees. Independent contractors are solely liable for their work and that of their employees unless the work is deemed hazardous. They often are contracted to perform a specific task during a defined time period for which they alone are responsible. The contracting employer does not control the work of the contractor beyond mere oversight. In fact, the more an employer directs the individual actions of an independent contractor, the more likely courts will find that an employment relationship exists rather than a contractual one. If a court finds an employment relationship because the employer began to direct the work of the contractor, then the employer becomes liable for the actions of the contractor/employee.

Employment of Minors

Many lifeguards begin their employment before the age of 18. These employees fall under the Department of Labor's rules for child employment. Hours that children may work are limited during the school year. Further, the specific tools that child employees may use are limited. Each state may implement additional state-specific laws and regulations that may be more restrictive than the federal child labor laws. Employers of children must be familiar with their state's requirements in addition to the federal laws because violations of child labor laws often carry heavy penalties.

Reducing Risk at Open-Water Races

In its January 2008 edition, *US News and World Report* revealed 50 top ways to improve your life in 2008. Number one on the list was open-water swimming. However, the increased popularity of open-water swimming comes with additional risks. In October 2010, 26-year-old Fran Crippen, a world-class, medal-winning athlete, died while competing in an open-water race in Dubai, United Arab Emirates. In part because it took more than two hours to discover his body, his tragic death has spurred a movement to make open-water swimming safer. Most open-water swimming tips found on the Internet deal with increased performance, however, not safety. After the sudden death of their fellow swimmer, scores of world-class swimmers called on FINA, the organization that oversees international swimming events, to tighten up its rules in order to ensure the safety of athletes in the open water.

These suggestions include allowing open-water swims only in water with temperatures between 18 and 28 degrees Celsius (64 to 82 °F). Other rec-ommendations cover water quality, rescue boats, transponders, finish funnels, feeding pontoons, and buoys.

For those competing in or organizing open-water swims in America, a good start is the United States Lifesaving Association, which published recommended guidelines for open-water swimming event safety in 2005. It should be noted that, during the writing of this text, many water safety experts were meeting to improve international open-water swimming competitions in light of Crippen's death. USLA outlines the minimum safety concepts that should be covered before and during the race. Following are some of these safety stipulations:

- The following personnel should be on hand: lifeguards trained by a recognized lifeguard training organization (e.g., ARC, USLA, StarGuard, YMCA), with CPR and first aid certifications; a swim safety coordinator; personal escorts, as necessary; a water-based law enforcement patrol; and a medical director.

- A water safety plan should be developed (USLA manual, chapters 16 and 17).

- A debriefing session should follow each event.

- Staffing levels are determined by considering the past experience for the same or similar events; number of participants; length of the course; design of the course; proximity of the swim course to shore; anticipated surf size; swimming ability of participants; presence or absence of a prequalifying swim; beach conditions; water temperature; currents; and weather conditions, including wind and fog.

- Races that exceed 2.5 miles (4 km) need personal escorts.

- The swim safety coordinator evaluates water and weather conditions before the race.

- Staff should be strategically placed throughout the race course.

- One EMT is required for every 150 participants.

- Medical evacuation from water to land should not exceed 10 minutes.

- A life support ambulance must be available on site (one ambulance per 250 swimmers).

- Radio communication between the aquatic safety coordinator and the medical group must be maintained throughout the event.
- A medical tent or shelter should be established for privacy.
- Each lifeguard along the race course must have an observation platform and rescue tube or buoy.
- Rescue boats are required for swim events conducted farther than 50 meters (15 feet) from shore.
- The communications system should include a public address system.
- A communications command center should be set up.
- Bright swim caps should be used for swimmer identification.
- Swimmers should be given a map of the swim course before the event.
- Wet suits are required when the water is below 60 degrees Fahrenheit (16 °C).
- A safety briefing should be held for all swimmers.
- Hand signals for lifeguards must be reviewed before the event.
- Rescue boat operators should receive instruction.
- An accountability system for identifying missing swimmers must be established.
- The course must be inspected for hazards, obstacles, and other problems.
- The course must be appropriately marked with buoys, markers, and anchor systems.
- Diving into shallow water is strictly prohibited.
- Wave starts are strongly recommended to reduce congestion, collisions, and harmful contact.
- Water quality should be tested and results posted.

For more comprehensive information regarding open-water swimming events, please refer to USLA's recommended minimum guidelines for open water swimming event safety. Contact www.USLA.org.

In addition to the strategies developed by USLA to safeguard swimmers during open-water events, technology is available that might also help. Just as there are drowning detection systems for swimming pools, there is now technology available to assist lifeguards in open-water swims. The Wahooo Swim Monitor System utilizes ultrasonic technology to track how long swimmers are underwater and alerts safety personnel if a swimmer is in distress. This dark-water drowning detection system works regardless of water visibility, and a locator device helps rescue personnel find the submerged swimmer. For more information, contact Wahooo Swim Monitor Systems at 888-439-9246 or www.wahooosms.com.

Summary

Managing a beach area in today's litigious environment requires an awareness of legal issues and an appreciation and understanding of the vital role a risk management plan plays in reducing liability. Most lawsuits for aquatic injuries involve a claim for negligence or are based on a theory of premises liability. Beach managers and their staff who act reasonably in protecting against foreseeable risks will go a long way toward avoiding lawsuits based on either theory. A risk management plan and consistent use of waivers, releases, and agreements to participate may not only prevent injuries but also discourage injured parties from filing suit. Last, managers must be aware of the important role human resources plays in avoiding liability for issues such as wrongful termination, discrimination, and violation of child labor laws. A commitment to safety and a common-sense approach to managing risks form the foundation of any well-administered aquatics program.

Effective Signage

Educating and Warning the Public

With contributions by Geoffrey Peckham
Clarion Safety Systems

⚠ **WARNING**

High surf.

Can cause serious injuries and drowning.

No swimming until further notice.

©Clarion Safety Systems, LLC · www.clarionsafety.com · Reorder No. HWS131-WSV-B6

The key to signage is to emphasize important warnings while minimizing less vital information. When it comes to accidents and lawsuits at beaches and waterfront facilities, personnel are often charged with failure to supervise or failure to warn. Whenever beaches and their attractions cannot be supervised, the obligation to warn effectively is of paramount importance. Educating guests is vitally important to increase the quality of their beach experience.

Most people spend only a few seconds reading signs, and numerous posted warnings compete for attention. When beaches post long lists of rules, regulations, and warnings, the end result is that little information gets conveyed to the reader. A great deal of information needs to be communicated to beachgoers, however. Most beach information, including rules and regulations, can be broken down into three major categories:

1. Information that must be known
2. Information that should be known
3. Information that is nice to know

For more than 10 years, Aquatic Safety Research Group has been developing a new system of effective safety signage for aquatic facilities, including waterfront areas. The major emphasis of this new safety signage system is to identify the greatest hazards and ways to avoid them, and sign them aggressively while separating and deemphasizing informational and directional signage. Streamlining signage should be the goal, with consistent sign design and colors for similar warnings. The objective is to educate and warn about catastrophic hazards and to inform and direct the public about other less important information without creating sign pollution.

In previous chapters we discussed the hazards found at beaches. The next step is to determine how to make the public aware of these hazards and what behaviors are expected. For example, beachgoers need to know where they can and cannot swim and be warned of hazards. This chapter gives background information on the harmonization of U.S. and international safety sign standards and defines the significant advances that are taking place with regard to beach and pool safety signs. We then discuss developing education and safety concepts that are intended to warn and protect the public. The objective is to educate beachgoers of the most important safety behaviors, in a concise and effective manner, before they enter the water.

Standards for Water Safety Signs

There's a new global language for visually communicating safety at the beach and in the water

sports environment. In August 2008, the International Organization for Standardization (ISO) published a new standard: *ISO 20712-1. Water safety signs and beach safety flags. Part 1. Specifications for water safety signs used in workplaces and public areas*. One of the major goals of ISO standards is that national standards be revised to incorporate ISO principles so that standardization of industry best practices and corresponding regulations occurs on a global basis. Over the past decade, standards harmonization has occurred throughout hundreds of industries. From a safety perspective, global standardization of visual systems for safety communication has taken on special emphasis (e.g., the UN-sponsored Globally Harmonized System for labeling hazardous chemicals, a system that incorporates standardized symbols and label formats). The new ISO standard for water safety signs was developed by experts from a multitude of countries including the United States.

The introduction to ISO 20712 states: "There is a need to standardize a system for giving safety information related to aquatic activity that relies as little as possible on the use of words to achieve understanding. Continued growth in international trade, travel, and mobility of labour requires a common method of communicating safety information. Lack of standardization may lead to confusion and perhaps accidents." Global standardization of the symbols contained in ISO 20712 is the objective so that water-related safety signs can be understood by people the world over. Since recreation and travel are often closely tied to the enjoyment of water-related activities (e.g., a vacation at the beach), safety signs for these areas have, as their target audience, practically every known nationality. Because it is foreseeable that people speaking a wide variety of different languages could be in the same location (e.g., a specific beach, resort, lake), a common global language of safety symbols for water-related risks and precautions is a practical necessity.

ISO 20712: Effectively Communicating Water Safety Information

ISO 20712 contains 50 graphical symbols, each appearing in one of three ISO-defined surround shapes for safety signs. Figure 5.1 shows the ISO

FIGURE 5.1a   A yellow triangle with a black band and black symbol signifies a warning sign, which is used to describe a hazard.

FIGURE 5.1b   A blue circle with a white symbol signifies a mandatory action sign, which is used to describe an action that needs to be taken to avoid a hazard.

FIGURE 5.1c   A red band with a red slash over a black symbol is a prohibition sign, which signifies an action not to be taken in order to avoid a hazard.

FIGURE 5.1d   A green square with a white symbol signifies a safe condition sign, which is used to communicate an area of safe conditions. A green square with a white symbol is also used to signify the location of safety equipment.

vocabulary of safety sign design as it pertains to water safety.

ANSI Z535.2: Formatting U.S. Safety Signs

In the United States, *ANSI Z535.2:2011 Environmental and Facility Safety Signs*, set by the American National Standards Institute, is the basis for defining what constitutes best practices in the area of safety signs. The Occupational Safety and Health Administration's safety sign regulation, 1910.144, was based on the precursors of the ANSI Z535.2 standard, the Z53.1:1968 and Z35.1:1970. Thus, the latest version of the ANSI Z535.2 standard is recognized by OSHA as the most up-to-date document related to the basis documents for their regulations.

ANSI Z535.2 differs from the 1968-era OSHA sign formats. The two major differences are (1) the ANSI standard used research and legal prec-

edent over the preceding three decades to better define the proper content of a safety sign (e.g., what the sign should communicate) and (2) the ANSI standard uses a better signal word and panel arrangement that more easily accommodates symbols and longer text messages. These changes reflect the best practices as defined by industry experience and the most up-to-date research in the area of warnings and instructions. The change in the signal word panel, first introduced in the 1998 version of the ANSI standard, uses a single system for the layout of safety signs, labels, and tags; the layout includes a signal word panel with standardized signal words for various levels of hazard severity recognition. This change to a single system, common for both product safety labels and facility and environmental safety signs, helps standardize the recognition of the level of severity for a safety sign or label wherever a person encounters one. Figure 5.2 shows the five signal word panels pertaining to accident prevention.

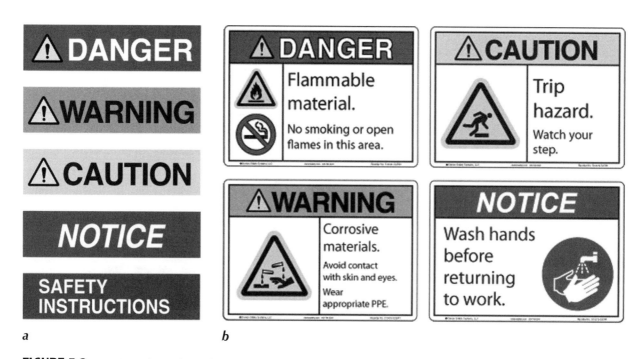

FIGURE 5.2 *(a)* Signal word panels and definitions from ANSI Z535.2:2011; *(b)* four typical safety signs designed according to ANSI Z535.2:2011.

In addition to the accident prevention signs that incorporate signal words, two additional formats are contained in the Z535.2 standard for the location of equipment, one for safety equipment and one for fire safety equipment (see figure 5.3).

Proper Content for Safety Signs

By moving toward the inclusion of fuller content, U.S. safety signs are following the liability-

FIGURE 5.3 Signs for location of safety equipment and fire equipment.

driven definition of an adequate warning as set by U.S. courts, the ANSI Z535 standards, and human factors research. Research conducted over the past decade has shown that compliance with a safety sign often hinges on the viewer's understanding of the hazard, the consequence of interaction with the hazard, the severity of the hazard, and knowing how to avoid the hazard. In product liability litigation, the courts have defined these four elements as the proper content of an adequate warning. Since the 1990s, the Z535 committee has adopted this definition as the proper content of a safety sign. The colored signal word panel defines the seriousness level, and text and symbols communicate the hazard nature, consequence, and avoidance information. The Z535.2 standard notes that one or more of the items of content may be omitted if they can be readily inferred—but such an assumption is wide sweeping, and from practical experience, we have found that the choice is usually made to include all content elements.

The use of text to repeat the meaning of the symbol is supported by the ISO. ISO 20712-1 encourages using text to supplement the graphical symbol to increase comprehension of the symbol and, in the longer term, to promote retention of the symbol's meaning. A good example is highway signs to indicate the location of services, which at one time typically used words (food, fuel, lodging, hospital). The move toward the use of symbols with words and then symbol-only signs has taken place on U.S. highways over the past decade (see figure 5.4).

The question of symbol-based signs is addressed in the ANSI Z535.2 standard in section 8.2:

> 8.2 Safety symbol use: Safety symbols may be used to clarify, supplement or substitute for a portion or all of a word message found in the message panel. A symbol may only be used to substitute for a portion or all of a word message if it has been demonstrated to be satisfactorily comprehended (e.g., Annex B of ANSI Z535.3) or there is a means (e.g., instructions, training materials,

manuals, etc.) to inform people of the symbol's meaning.

Thus, the ANSI Z535.2 standard does allow the use of symbol-based signs in the United States in a qualified way; the symbols must be shown to be satisfactorily comprehended or there must be a way to inform people of their meaning, and they must be accompanied by a signal word panel. This is important to note because the USLA may want to consider an implementation methodology that posts symbol-only signs (with signal words) and has a set of "know your symbols" or "know your safety signs" training signs that define each symbol's meaning in a variety of languages (these signs would presumably be posted in central locations so visitors have the opportunity to become trained in the meaning of the symbol-based signs).

FIGURE 5.4 Current U.S. highway service signs.

Integrating ISO 20712 with ANSI Z535.2

Figure 5.5 shows an example of the old safety sign format for beaches. This design uses the circa 1968 ASA Z53.1 format for the signal word panel made obsolete in 2002 by the ANSI Z535.2 standard. It also uses safety symbols that have been replaced by the new ISO 20712-2:2008 standard.

FIGURE 5.5 Old-style beach and water safety sign with text and symbol.

Figure 5.6 illustrates three ways that the newer ANSI Z535.2 and ISO standards can be combined to form a new best practice for water safety signs for the United States. Each set of signs is followed by a summary of the pros and cons of each style. All three sets of signs use the newer ANSI Z535.2 signal word panels and the new ISO 20712-2:2008 symbols. You will note that, given the previous discussion, all three format options are allowed by ANSI. The benefits of each type of format may change over time. For example, as people become educated on the meaning of the symbols, text may become less necessary.

Establishing Shoreline Zones

Simply posting signs to educate and warn guests does not adequately protect them. Identifying areas and directing beachgoers in the right direction to keep them safe are also important. Symbols, letters, and numbers can be significant when labeling and describing beaches. After you have identified the various hazards and features of a potential beach area, as well as determined the appropriate use of the area, the next step is to establish shoreline zones. Many bodies of water have diverse ownership and accessibility issues along the shoreline. For safety in and around the water and to better control safe access to the shoreline, the shoreline needs to be identified, described, and clearly labeled as to the types of activities compatible with its different areas.

Separate and distinct zones should be created to increase safety and reduce conflicts between boaters, fishermen, surfers, waders, and so on. Tall, strong poles with the appropriate identifying colors should be placed around the shoreline. Tall poles are more effective than the shorter signs that now clutter many waterfronts. Signs explaining the color-coding system and safe water practices still need to be posted, but this should be part of an overall effort to channel recreators to major access points to more effectively educate and warn the public. Literature pertaining to the recreational use of the open water should show the entire shoreline, color coded according to the zones described as follows, to show beach users where particular recreational uses are authorized.

FIGURE 5.6 Combining Standards to Form a New Practice for Water Safety Signs

Pros: These signs incorporate text and symbols for both sections of the message: hazard description and hazard avoidance. The text reinforces both symbols. People who do not speak English will be able to use both symbols to understand the critical parts of the safety message.

Cons: This approach requires a larger sign.

Pros: These signs use only a single symbol, the hazard description symbol, and English text. The sign is compact in size. Text and symbol combine to communicate a full safety message.

Cons: Non-English-speaking audiences may miss out on the hazard avoidance message. The sign relies on the hazard description symbol to adequately imply what the avoidance step should be.

Pros: The symbol-only approach is intended to communicate the entire sign message to all audiences, functioning much like highway service location signs. Smaller sign dimensions are the result of this approach.

Cons: The symbols may need to be reinforced with training materials in order for them to be comprehended. This may be an approach to graduate to after signs with symbols *and* text have been used for a period of time.

Closed Shoreline: (Color Code: Orange and Black)

Dangerous to pedestrians and waders. The geology, topography, and underwater hazards make it dangerous for anyone to access the lake from these areas, and appropriate signage is necessary: "Danger: Hidden hazards—do not go near the water." An oval danger sign often used to indicate high voltage is suggested in this area.

Approved Boating Access (Color Code: Blue and White)

These areas are recommended for safe boating access, whether the shoreline is publicly or privately owned. Appropriate signage regarding boating rules and regulations should be maintained. Safety equipment (e.g., throw bag or ring buoy, fire station pull box) may also be available at public boating access points. Kiosks or information boards containing boating safety information, particularly information regarding alcohol use while boating, are highly recommended. Boaters must be educated with appropriate signage as they are directed or channeled to boat launches. Private and public launches should follow the same recommendations and rules.

Approved Fishing Access (Color Code: Brown and White)

Fishing access should also be controlled. Fishing areas should be relatively close to wading and boating areas but safely segregated. Lifesaving equipment (e.g., throw bag or ring buoy) should be maintained at these access points. Fishing should not be permitted after hours within designated wading areas.

Approved Wading Access (Color Code: Green and White)

Wading is defined as walking in the water to a depth no greater than waist deep. Waders should be instructed to have one foot on the bottom at all times and to not submerge beneath the surface. If water quality monitoring programs are not in place, it is advisable to post a sign indicating the lack of a water quality program: "Caution: Bacteria levels not monitored. For your safety, keep your head above water at all times." United States Coast Guard–approved personal flotation devices (lifejackets) should be worn by nonswimmers in these areas. Parents must be urged to actively supervise their young waders from the water, not the beach.

This beach pole not only illustrates the acceptable activities allowed at this beach but also serves as a family meeting place, complete with emergency phone. The beach pole is numbered for faster emergency response.

Placing Beach Flags for Safety Zone Conditions

Beach flags are becoming more popular throughout the world, particularly at surf beaches. Although many experts agree with the beach flag concept, changing the colored flags in a timely fashion can be troublesome, particularly in areas where weather and water conditions are so unpredictable. Another potential problem with beach flags is that lifeguards often are required to take the flags down when they leave for the day. Many drowning deaths occur after hours when both lifeguards and flags are absent. Perhaps a special flag or sign is needed to discourage swimmers from entering the water after hours, particularly when water conditions are dangerous.

Flags to Identify Water Quality

One option is to use an appropriately striped flagpole from which could fly a colored water quality flag. Such flag systems have been met with much success at both freshwater and marine beaches worldwide. Red flags are often used to indicate no swimming because of high bacteria levels. Blue flags generally indicate acceptable bacteria levels as of the date of the last test. Blue flags (and Blue Flag awards) are used in Europe and South Africa to indicate clean water that has passed bacteria standards (see www.blueflag.org /Criteria/EuropeanBeaches). In some states, such as Kansas, blue flags are used to indicate clean water, while green flags indicate water is safe for recreation activities, *but* persons should shower if they've had full contact with the water, should avoid swallowing the water, and should wash their hands before eating or drinking. However, these are advisable regardless of bacteria levels and should be part of a general education campaign regarding water quality issues.

Flags to Identify Surf Conditions

The water quality flag system should not be confused with a beach warning flag system often used at marine beaches to indicate surf conditions. Most beach flag advocates recommend the traffic light color scheme (red, yellow, and green).

The green flag means calm, relatively safe conditions for swimming and wading. The key to an effective beach flag system is timely changing of the flags as the water conditions vary.

Double red: water closed to public
Red: high hazard
Yellow: medium hazard
Green: low hazard
Purple: marine pest present

Channeling the Public to Beach Access Points

Aggressive safety signage is a vitally important service for all beach visitors, but even the best signs will be ineffective if they are not read because the public is not drawn to them. With appropriate landscaping, fences, and barriers, the public—particularly families with young children—can be better warned and educated as they are channeled to approved shoreline points that have been inspected for safety. Approved access points are recommended instead of attempting to place signage in a repeated manner across

an entire beachfront. Providing easy access for persons with disabilities during this channeling process is of paramount importance.

Once shoreline zones and access points are identified, one option is to put in place a numbering system for each access area. The numbers should be consecutive and continue along the perimeter of the shoreline to the last numbered access point. For an inland body of water, the system of numbering should rotate clockwise around the waterfront. No distinction in the number system should be made between the shoreline zones and types of access points (wading, fishing, boating, closed access, and so on). This numbering system allows for a coordinated and timely response from the local emergency services (police, fire, EMS) because all zones are numbered for identification and follow a numerical pattern around the shoreline rather than randomly assigned numbers for each area. A tall telephone-type pole or PVC pole striped with the zone color should be placed in a central location, prominently displaying the access point

Lake Elsinore spent a great amount of time, effort, and money to enhance shoreline safety by improving and channeling guests through select entry points for better education and warnings.

number on an appropriately colored sign (blue, green, brown, or orange). These beach poles can also be used as family meeting places should children become separated from their parents. Emergency pull boxes or call boxes and basic water rescue equipment could also be placed on or near these poles.

Functional and friendly access to the beach can be accomplished through a variety of ways including fences, landscaping that cannot be breached, berms, and other physical barriers. Whether driving, biking, or walking to the beach, guests should eventually be guided through a few central pedestrian paths, walkovers, or entrances so that each and every guest can be effectively and efficiently educated about safe and enjoyable ways to use the beach.

An information kiosk that is weatherproof and vandal proof should also be placed at most entrances. These kiosks can help convey advisories and public education materials. Likewise, boaters should be warned and educated as they are channeled or funneled to their launches.

Using Access Points to Warn and Educate

If you strategically position aggressive warning signs that are designed properly and not camouflaged in long lists of rules and regulations, it would be difficult for guests to claim ignorance. People who have been injured at the beach often claim they were unaware the hazard existed or that they did not see the warning signs.

Hazard signs and other warnings particular to certain beaches are of paramount importance and should be placed at each entrance. Danger and warning signs at beach entry points should be emphasized over other rules and regulations (e.g., directions and behaviors that are not life threatening), should be larger and more conspicuous than other signage, and should use appropriate warning shapes and colors. Borrowing from the highway signs is an excellent idea in this regard.

Universal Warnings

Of all the rules, regulations, and information needing to be signed at beaches, there are five very important warnings that apply universally to just about all beaches:

1. Parents, please supervise your children closely and constantly.
2. No diving or other headfirst entries.
3. No breath holding or prolonged underwater swimming.
4. Nonswimmers should always wear a lifejacket.
5. Warning: Hidden hazards. (Include beach-specific hazards here: rip currents, dangerous marine life, and so on.)

At most swimming beaches, all other information falls far below the significance and timeliness of these four major safety concerns. These warnings are also important for reminding individuals and families of their responsibility to behave in a way that reduces the likelihood of an injury or drowning. Beaches can simply, inexpensively, and effectively post these five warnings conspicuously in parking lots, at the beach entrances, and on the back of lifeguard stations.

Warn to Supervise Children

Unfortunately, parents do not realize how quickly a drowning can occur. It takes only seconds for a child to drown, some estimates stating that drowning can occur in as little as 90 seconds.

Adults are often lax in supervision, thinking their supervision is adequate if they are in the general area and occasionally checking where their children are. If parents are not in the

The Five Cs of Signage

The five Cs of signage can be used effectively to better communicate important information to the public:

Creative: Develop clever, meaningful messages that your audience can relate to.

Clear: Test the clarity of your signs with staff and guests before posting them.

Concise: Keep messages simple and to the point. Use few words, and add international symbols.

Conspicuous: Place the most important signs where they will be read, and channel people around these signs if possible. Place signs slightly above the eye level of most of your patrons. Consider the "three strike" rule which means beachgoers pass by the warnings three times before they enter the water (parking lot, entrance, restrooms or lifeguard stations). Choose suitable locations for posting information. As an example, signs banning inflatable devices are most appropriate in parking areas and on printed materials because the goal is to prevent patrons from bringing the inflatable devices to the beach rather than to ask them to bring inflatables back to their cars.

Consistent: Develop a scheme that uses standard best practices in terms of color, shape, and symbols for the information you wish to convey.

water with children who are weak swimmers or nonswimmers, and they are not within arm's reach, they are not actively supervising their children.

Distressed nonswimmers can slip beneath the surface of the water in as little as 20 seconds and without warning. Once a child slips below the surface of the water, drowning occurs silently. Although many parents supervise their children passively at home, when it comes to safety in, on, or around the water, children must be supervised both actively and aggressively. Messages such as "If you're more than an arm's length away, you've gone too far"; "Two seconds is too long"; and "It only takes seconds for a child to drown" are important safety messages that have been used throughout North America. All waterfronts should adopt a safety campaign to educate the public that children of tender years must be closely guarded around the water.

Warn Against Headfirst Entries

Approximately 800 to 900 catastrophic neck injuries resulting in permanent paralysis (quadriplegia or paraplegia) or death are caused by ill-advised headfirst entries into shallow water. Of these injuries, most result in death. Most serious neck injuries occur in open water rather than in swimming pools or from diving boards. Approximately two-thirds of all catastrophic neck injuries occur in open-water environments (Griffiths

2003). Running down a beach and then diving headfirst into shallow water is a classic recipe for a catastrophic neck injury. Particularly when both turbid and shallow water exist, catastrophic neck injuries are a very real hazard. Additionally, many people believe the longer a dock extends into the water, the deeper the water is, and as a result, diving is safe from the end of most docks. Of course, this is not necessarily true, and someone's poor judgment in this regard can result in serious injury or death.

Aggressive warnings prohibiting headfirst entries from beaches, docks, piers, and other structures into open water are clearly necessary. "No diving" signs with a "no diving" international graphic logo should be posted strategically. "No diving" should also be posted directly onto the horizontal planks and vertical posts of all docks, piers, and jetties. Because most diving injuries involve alcohol consumption, a serious yet creative sign campaign could state "Drinking and diving do not mix."

Warn Against Prolonged Breath Holding

Competitive breath holding, repetitive breath holding, and underwater swimming can be deadly by creating shallow-water blackout scenarios that can cause either drowning or sudden death from cardiac arrhythmia. Although shallow-water blackouts are more common in traditional competitive swimming pools, they do occur in

The good news here is that these children are wearing lifejackets. The bad news is that an adult supervisor is not in the water with them. Particularly at beaches, if parents are more than an arm's length from their child, they have gone too far.

the open water, especially when free divers or surfers are trapped under waves. When someone blacks out under the surface of the water, the limited visibility of natural water makes recovery and successful resuscitation almost impossible. Swimmers should be warned against prolonged underwater swimming and competitive and repetitive breath holding.

Warn Nonswimmers to Wear a Lifejacket

Warning nonswimmers to wear a lifejacket may be the most proactive and effective of all warnings. Even with the most conscientious parents and vigilant lifeguards on duty, nonswimmers continue to drown because of momentary lapses in concentration or distractions. Tragically, many young children drown in "safer" shallow water less than 5 feet deep. An appropriately-fitting Coast Guard-approved lifejacket is perhaps the best insurance policy against drowning. The water safety culture must be changed from using lifejackets exclusively in boats to using lifejackets in all bodies of water. Strong signage educating guests about the need for lifejackets will help in this regard. Lifejackets should be required for all bodies of water for nonswimming children under 48 inches tall. Loaner lifejacket programs are also an excellent idea (see page 87 for more information).

Warn of the Hazards of Open Waters

Many people do not appreciate that the water in oceans, lakes, rivers, and ponds quickly hides and suffocates people who slip below the surface. Open water is often not crystal clear or clean enough to drink, and it is much more hazardous than waters found in treated and filtered swimming pools and water parks. Most people also fail to understand that swallowing water containing elevated bacteria levels can make them sick with gastrointestinal illnesses. Of greatest concern are young children, the elderly, or anyone with compromised immune systems (such as those undergoing cancer treatment or living with HIV, the human immunodeficiency virus), for whom gastrointestinal illnesses can become life threatening.

Waterfronts should also warn of any hidden dangers that exist under the water within designated swimming and wading areas, including sudden drop-offs or inshore holes. Where plant life is abundant, swimmers should be warned of their presence and instructed to swim slowly through them to avoid panic. Where shorebreak or rip currents exist, warning signs should be posted.

In rivers where dangerous conditions exist, the best way to prevent deaths is by placing several layers of protection upstream. Aggressive signage on the riverbanks; signs and flags strung across and above the river; and large, buoyant lines or booms on the surface of the river, upstream of a low-head dam whenever possible, could all be effective in saving lives. Low-head dams must be aggressively marked and signed to keep the public clearly away from harm's reach.

Beach signs need to follow a consistent graphical standard. "Our ocean/lake/river is beautiful but can be dangerous"; "These waters may be deep, dark, and dangerous"; and "Underwater hazards exist. Please use extreme caution" are all important messages that should be conveyed regularly to the public.

Site-Specific Warnings

When designing a signage program to better communicate important information, remember that signs should be creative, clear, and specific to the environment. Prefabricated signs not customized to meet the needs of a particular shoreline may go unnoticed or unappreciated by beach users. The sample signs included in this chapter are intended to help illustrate key points and should not be considered endorsed or approved signs. Selected sample images, language, and design specifications should be adapted to local needs.

Warn That No Lifeguards Are on Duty

Unguarded beaches have an even greater responsibility to prominently post the five universal warnings, with the additional warning that no lifeguards are on duty. Strong warnings at unguarded beaches are preferred, such as "Warning: Unguarded and unpatrolled beach. Hidden hazards" or "No lifeguards on duty."

When feasible, informing beachgoers of the location of the nearest guarded beach would be beneficial in terms of offering a safer swimming option. Insisting that guests refrain from solo swimming is also an important safety message. Using the beach with a partner who can swim could save a life. Above all, people swimming or wading at unguarded beaches must be reminded to exercise good judgment and common sense.

Warn When Conditions Change

When there are a multitude of environmental hazards, including currents and dangerous marine life, signs may need to be changed as conditions change. A flag warning system that is readily changeable may be preferable to permanent signs. Other information that is necessary at the beach can be downgraded to secondary importance, reduced in size and significance, and placed in a somewhat less conspicuous place once the universal warnings are prioritized.

Warn Against Excessive Alcohol Consumption

The heat, the water, and time off from work all contribute to excessive alcohol consumption in, on, and around the recreation area. Alcohol consumption is often linked to drowning, diving injuries, boating accidents, and a lack of supervision over young children. Perhaps signs such as "Alcohol and aquatics do not mix" or "Water and alcohol do not mix" should be posted at all access points to discourage alcohol consumption and educate about the consequences of drinking and recreating around the lake. Knowing that most boating accidents involve alcohol consumption, signs specific to state laws and regulations regarding alcohol consumption and boating should be considered at boating access points. Cooperatively campaigning with beer and liquor manufacturers should help in this regard.

Warn Against Swimming or Wading

Yellow diamond warning signs indicating "No swimming" or "No wading" should be placed in approved recreation areas where swimming or wading is not allowed.

These signs should not, however, be placed on closed shorelines, where access to the lake is banned. Placing no swimming, no wading, and no diving signs where pedestrian traffic is banned could have the unfortunate result of actually encouraging these dangerous activities in areas where they are restricted. Again, a consistent and creative approach to water safety signage is needed.

Many pools and beaches warn swimmers and waders that swimming or wading is at their own risk. This type of statement often sends the wrong message and actually serves as an invitation to swim or wade, running counter to the local ordinance prohibiting swimming. When swimming and wading need to be discouraged, a more aggressive warning is needed. "Danger: Do not enter the water" or "Use extreme caution" may be more appropriate and more effective. Moreover, wherever boaters, waders, and pedestrians frequent the same areas from different directions such as access walkways, piers and levees, and boats or personal watercraft, two-sided signs should be used so that everyone reads the same messages.

Prioritizing the Safety Message

Prioritizing certain rules and proper placement of signs that convey these rules will help make beach signage strategies more effective.

A major problem in aquatics, including beaches, is that we attempt to convey three distinctly different types of information simultaneously and haphazardly. It is almost impossible to find a beach that does not include scores of rules on signs posted on and around the beach. Consider just a few of the rules and regulations posted at beaches: "No glass," "No pets," "No food or drink," "No diving," "No smoking," "No profanities," "No ball throwing." To make matters worse, most of these rules are found on the same rectangular sign. Unfortunately, "must know" information is often lost among the "should know" and "nice to know" information. Beach managers should concentrate on information that must be communicated and deemphasize, rather than eliminate, the other two categories.

Beaches need to make their first signage priority warnings against catastrophic injuries. Such warnings should be made larger and use appropriately shaped signs and colors. Warnings about noncatastrophic concerns can and should be deemphasized somewhat because they clutter the beach landscape and take away from more important issues. Informational and directional colors should be used for noncatastrophic issues that tend to be more housekeeping and behavioral in nature. For example, stepping on broken glass can cause an ugly wound and may even lead to a lawsuit, but it will not nearly approach the problems resulting from someone doing a headfirst dive into shallow water. Likewise, eating and drinking on the beach may create unsightly litter, but it will not have the same dire consequences as parents who do not carefully supervise their children around the water. Regardless of where the beach is located or what type of beach it is, parents not carefully supervising their children, headfirst entries, prolonged competitive and repetitive breath holding, and environmental beach hazards can quickly lead to loss of life or debilitating injuries.

Posting and Distributing Healthy Swimming Information

Educational signage should be placed conspicuously in appropriate areas (e.g., near parking lots and restrooms) to provide beach patrons with information about healthy swimming. Educate the public about drowning prevention and sun protection. Figure 5.7 describes a safe beach campaign launched at the beaches of South Walton, Florida.

Drowning Prevention

The American Red Cross states approximately 60 percent of those who drown in the United States never even intended to get wet, and most people who drown did not know how to swim. Waterfronts, in cooperation with local schools, national water safety training agencies, or other concerned organizations, should begin a drowning prevention program for parents and children alike. This drowning prevention program should have three approaches:

FIGURE 5.7 Seven Tips for Family Beach Safety

1. Keep kids within arm's reach (especially in the sea, but also on land).
2. Don't dive in (two-thirds of catastrophic neck, head, and spinal injuries occur in open-water areas).
3. Knee deep is too deep (strong winds, waves, and currents create dangerous rip currents that can sweep a child out to sea).
4. Know before you go (know your beach flags: red means stop, green means go).
5. Take frequent breaks (every hour take a sun, bathroom, or water break).
6. Go with the wind (lost kids tend to take the course of least resistance: follow the wind to find your child).
7. Look but don't touch (call local authorities to help injured or stranded animals).

Based on Walton County Tourist Development Council. Available: www.SeemoreSafetyCrab.com.

1. Teach people to swim or at least encourage them to learn how to swim.
2. Offer water safety programs—specifically dealing with local beaches—in schools, libraries, parks, YMCAs, Boy Scouts, Girl Scouts, and so on.
3. Offer waterfront water safety seminars during the summer months, particularly on the weekends.

In addition to the safety information presented here, elementary forms of rescue should be discussed. The best approach for water rescue is the "reach, row, throw, but do not go" philosophy, emphasizing the basic rescue devices found at the beach (e.g., ring buoy, reaching pole, throw line). First and foremost, waterfront communities should encourage all residents to learn how to swim. By partnering with other agencies that maintain swimming pools, waterfront communities could offer free or low-cost lessons to children and adults. If swimming pools are not easily accessible, future consideration should be given to partnering with local agencies to build a pool. Education programs both in the schools and at the beach could be provided by beach staff, police, and fire and rescue personnel as well as many other people. Senior citizens can even be used in this capacity. The Army Corps of Engineers uses park rangers to provide education programs at their lakeside swimming beaches throughout the country. The ideal water safety lecture of this type should last 30 to 45 minutes.

It cannot be overemphasized that wearing lifejackets in and around the water is extremely important for preventing drowning in nonswimmers. Lifejackets should not be reserved exclusively for use in boats; they should be worn at beaches, pools, and water parks as well. For additional drowning prevention strategies, a great resource is the National Drowning Prevention Alliance (www.NDPA.org).

Protection From the Sun

Too much sun exposure, particularly in childhood, can lead to chronic skin problems including melanoma. Protecting yourself and your children from harmful UV rays and exercising safe practices in the sun are important for long-term health and safety. Today, one out of seven people is likely to develop some type of skin cancer.

Scientists and medical experts have determined that ultraviolet (UV) radiation causes sunburn, skin aging, cataracts, and skin cancer. It also exacerbates the symptoms of lupus. To help people understand and respond to the potential dangers of UV rays, the UV Index was introduced in a number of countries in 1995 and 1996. In the United States, it is published on a daily basis and provides an estimate of the maximum potential hazard from UV rays for the next day. Table 5.1 offers interpretations and recommended actions for the UV Index developed by the Environmental Protection Agency.

Many people believe skin cancer is a relatively harmless condition—when a mole or blemish appears, they can simply visit the doctor, have it removed, and life goes on with no problems. However, approximately 10,000 Americans die each year as a result of skin cancer. Approximately 8,000 of these deaths are from malignant melanoma, while the remaining 2,000 deaths mostly resulted from squamous cell carcinomas. The

TABLE 5.1 Recommended Actions for the UV Index

Exposure category	UV Index	General recommended action (all skin types)
Minimal	0, 1, 2	Apply SPF 15+ sunscreen.
Low	3, 4	Apply SPF 15+ sunscreen; wear protective clothing including a hat.
Moderate	5, 6	Apply SPF 15+ sunscreen; wear protective clothing including a hat and protective sunglasses.
High	7, 8, 9	Apply SPF 15+ sunscreen; wear protective clothing including a hat and protective sunglasses; avoid the sun between 10:00 a.m. and 4:00 p.m.
Very high	10+	Apply SPF 15+ sunscreen; wear protective clothing including a hat and protective sunglasses; avoid the sun between 10:00 a.m. and 4:00 p.m.

Sunscreen Tips

For sunscreen to do its job, it must be applied correctly. Be sure to do the following:

- Apply sunscreen whenever you will be in the sun.
- Apply sunscreen about 30 minutes before going outside so that a good layer of protection can form. Don't forget about lips, hands, ears, feet, shoulders, and behind the neck. Lift up bathing suit straps and apply sunscreen underneath them (in case the straps shift as you move).
- Don't try to stretch out a bottle of sunscreen; apply it generously.
- Reapply sunscreen often, approximately every two to three hours, as recommended by the American Academy of Dermatology. Reapply after sweating or swimming.
- Apply a waterproof sunscreen whenever you are around water or swimming. Water reflects and intensifies the sun's rays, so those immersed in water still need protection that lasts. Waterproof sunscreens may last up to 80 minutes in the water, and some are also sweat- and rub-proof. But regardless of the waterproof label, be sure to reapply sunscreen whenever you and your family come out of the water.

biggest danger is letting skin cancer go untreated. Whenever you are uncertain about a mole or freckle that has changed in some way, you should always have it examined by a physician.

Just as layers of protection can safeguard against drowning, so too does this concept apply to safeguarding beachgoers against the harmful UV rays of the sun. Most people accumulate between 50 and 80 percent of their lifetime sun exposure before age 18, so it's important that parents teach their children how to safely enjoy fun in the sun. But parents are also susceptible to skin cancer and must set a good example by protecting themselves from the sun as well. With the right precautions, you can greatly reduce the risk that you or your children will develop skin cancer. Appropriate hats covering the head, neck, and ears are important along with sun-protective clothing (which incorporates special UV-blocking fabrics), SPF lotions, umbrellas, and other shade structures. Following are some tips to keep safe in the sun:

- Avoid the strongest rays of the sun during the day (typically between 10:00 a.m. and 4:00 p.m.).
- Cover up completely, preferably with sun-protective clothing and hats.
- Use sunscreen (UVA and UVB, 15 SPF or greater) liberally and consistently.
- Wear appropriate eyewear that blocks UV rays, preferably Polaroid.

- Check medications to be certain they do not cause a sensitivity to sun exposure.
- Infants under six months old should not wear sunscreen. Keep them fully clothed, including a sun hat, or in the shade.

When it comes to protecting beachgoers from the harmful effects of overexposure to the sun, beach managers should provide educational information about sun protection at information kiosks, bulletin boards, and restrooms. In addition, whenever possible, provide shade structures for guests at the beach so they do not have to leave the beach completely to get a reprieve from the sun.

Summary

The ISO safety sign vocabulary of surround shape and color for the graphical symbols for safety messages is fast gaining worldwide acceptance in a wide variety of industries. Such a global approach to communicating safety makes sense, especially for beaches and hotel or resort swimming pools, where it's expected that people from various national backgrounds will be the intended audiences for these critical safety messages. In the coming years it will be incumbent on the United States to integrate the ISO vocabulary of safety symbols into signs formatted to the current ANSI Z535.2 formats for environmental and facility safety signs in order to achieve effective safety communication. In addition, since these safety symbols and sign formats are compliant with the latest best practice standards, they will also be held up in court as setting the standard of care for the duty to warn associated with property liability exposure. It is thus incumbent on state, municipal, and private owners of beach, water park, and pool facilities to upgrade their water safety signs in accordance with these best prac-tices in order to reduce risk and protect the lives of people using those facilities. Educating guests is key and can be accomplished through a variety of ways including designated poles and informa-tion kiosks. Using a variety of media increases the effectiveness of your education efforts. There are numerous excellent drowning prevention programs and sun protection strategies that will help enhance safety at your beach.

Nonswimming Beach Safety

Hans Vogelsong
East Carolina University

In the book *Moby Dick* by Herman Melville, the author states that "meditation and the water are wedded forever." This statement remains true today. Water can be mesmerizing, promoting deep thought and relaxation. That is why so many people seek homes and offices with a view of the water. Waterfronts can improve the quality of life for people who do not recreate in or on these bodies of water. It is important to know how to deal with all bodies of water, whether or not they were designed for active recreation.

59

As mentioned throughout this book, waterfronts and beaches are highly attractive areas to people. Water provides many fun activities, a place to cool off on a hot day, and a sense of serenity, and it attracts a variety of wildlife to watch and feed. However, there are many times when people want to enjoy the water from a distance rather than get into it. This chapter discusses some of the reasons it may not be conducive for guests and residents to get in the water and provides some suggestions on how to keep them safe and dry.

Reasons for Keeping People Out of the Water

Beaches and waterfront areas may be closed to the public temporarily, seasonally, or permanently. There are a variety of reasons for not wanting the general public to wade or swim at waterfronts and beaches. The following are common reasons why it may be important to keep people out of the water.

Lack of Supervision

Certainly not all beaches and waterfronts provide water supervision in the form of lifeguards, and many that do provide it only seasonally and in some areas of a waterway. Although not all beaches are guarded, many agencies have policies stating that only supervised water will be available to the public for swimming and wading.

Pollution

Pollution from both point and nonpoint sources can cause water to be unfit for human contact on either a short-term or long-term basis. Point pollution is when the pollutant is discharged directly into flowing water sources, whereas as nonpoint sources are pollutants running off lawns, driveways, roadways, and parking lots that enter our waterways indirectly. Harmful bacteria from agricultural waste, sanitary sewers, chemical spills, industrial discharge, and other sources can make water unfit for human contact for a period of many years. Furthermore, floods and other natural disasters can introduce dangerous pollutants from the same sources that make water unsafe on a short-term basis. Passing ships

and careless acts have also been known to introduce marine debris such as packing materials, commercial fishing gear and nets, timbers, and plastics into waters, causing unsafe conditions to swim and wade in.

Dangerous Currents

Swift currents, eddies, and turbulence create unpredictable and dangerous conditions that swimmers should avoid. These can be the result of flooding, human-made hazards such as the tailwaters of dams and water control projects, or permanent natural hazards in some waterways. Additionally, rip currents in oceans and bays often produce similar conditions. Regardless of the source of these hazards, currents are capable of creating deadly situations for even the strongest and most experienced swimmers.

Rocks and Other Obstructions

Rocks, downed trees, old fences, and uneven bottom conditions, occurring in many lakes, streams, and rivers, make being in the water hazardous to swimmers. The fact that many of these objects are submerged and cannot be seen makes them especially dangerous to divers. Combined

Although the shores of Lake Michigan can be beautifully calm and serene, at times the lake can be deadly dangerous. Therefore, signage is needed to warn about the hidden and unexpected dangers that may occur in these waters.

with swift currents, both submerged and visual obstructions can create deadly hazards that swimmers can strike or become ensnared in.

Resource Protection

Although not as common a cause as those already listed, resource protection has also been documented as a reason to keep swimmers and waders out of the water. Endangered species of flora and fauna are often found in aquatic areas and may be disturbed by swimmers and waders. Additionally, too many people at a particular site can lead to ground compaction and shoreline erosion. Finally, many water impoundments are used as a source for drinking water and should not be contaminated by swimmers and waders.

Obviously, there are many reasons why an agency responsible for the stewardship of a shoreline (creek, river, lake, or ocean) may want to keep the public out of the water. Regardless of the exact reason, more and more beach and water closures are occurring each year as technology provides us with easier and more efficient ways to identify hazards to both humans and aquatic species. However, the real trick to managing these sites is to provide a setting that is welcoming to the public but that also encourages them to stay dry. The remainder of this chapter focuses on tactics that agencies can employ to keep the public out of the water.

Methods to Keep People Out of the Water

When the public attempt to get in the water at beaches and waterfronts where we want to keep them dry, we can classify these actions as undesirable visitor behavior. Most of the research on deterring undesirable visitor behavior categorizes such efforts as either direct or indirect. Direct methods are sometimes thought to be heavy handed in that they do not provide people with a choice of how they behave, whereas indirect methods are designed to manipulate visitors to behave in a manner that is acceptable. Examples of direct methods include creating and enforcing rules and physically preventing people from entering the water through the use of fences, barriers, and enclosures. Examples of indirect methods include manipulating people by changing their attitudes about entering the water through educational efforts or by changing site

characteristics to make entering the water less desirable or more difficult.

Posting Signs

Signs can be an effective way to keep people out of the water provided they include adequate information. Very simple signs that merely say "Keep out" or "No swimming and wading" are not as effective as signs that convey those messages as well as the reasons for them. Remember that signs are meant to be communication tools, so the more information they include about specific hazards or reasons for the public to stay out of the water, the more effective they are likely to be. Messages that include warnings ("Danger") as well as consequences ("Possible injury or death") greatly increase the value of the signs as a risk management tool and help the public understand why you do not want them in the water. See chapter 5 for more information about proper signage.

Disseminating Educational Materials

Like signage, education is a communication tool that can be effective in convincing the public to behave in a particular manner. Educational methods of keeping people out of the water take many different forms including public announcements, brochures, positive public relations, environmental education, information kiosks, and interpretive displays. The idea behind this type of education is to provide the visiting public with information that will convince them to stay out of the water on their own. Therefore messages must be persuasive enough to be effective and should be targeted at specific audiences.

In some cases, different educational messages may be required for different sectors of the public, and at times the messages may require changing. For example, after the flooding caused by Hurricane Floyd in North Carolina in December 2007, several public service announcements were sent out to stop people from attempting to bathe and wash clothing in the flooded Tar River. Although messages focusing on dangerous currents and harmful bacteria did little to convince the public to stay out of the river, an announcement stating that poisonous snakes were inhabiting the water almost completely curbed this undesirable behavior.

It is also important to consider where and when to focus the education efforts. Although providing on-site brochures stating your waterfront areas are nonswimming may keep people out of the water, those who showed up planning to go swimming are not likely to be happy when they receive the news. Furthermore, many people will not stop in the visitor center or read materials on information kiosks before heading straight for the water. Some people must simply be reached before their visit to ensure they are aware of rules and conditions before they arrive. Efforts should be made to provide consistent educational materials as public service announcements, in brochures available through district offices, and on the Internet to help give visitors accurate expectations. This is especially important when managing beaches and waterfront areas that are closed to swimmers only on a seasonal basis.

Many natural areas and state parks containing nonswimming beaches provide an array of environmental education and interpretation programs to educate the public on a wide range of issues. These can be especially effective because a great deal of information can be conveyed through face-to-face contact, and the programs can be flexible enough to make this information relevant to a variety of audiences. For example, during a program on turtles, an interpretive ranger can weave in information describing how nests, newborn turtles, and important food sources can all be negatively affected by swimmers and waders, and the best way to help protect this species is to simply stay out of the water. Furthermore, interpretive signs and displays can be created on the shore featuring animals perceived to be dangerous (e.g., snakes, alligators, sharks)

This walking trail sits on the precipice paralleling the Niagara River just below Niagara Falls. A substantial railing system is needed to prevent a catastrophic fall into the turbulent river below.

or focusing on fragile ecosystems. In any case, it is important to note that education as a tool is not meant to take a heavy-handed (direct) approach to keep people out of the water but is intended to manipulate people into making acceptable behavioral decisions.

Erecting Fences, Barriers, and Enclosures

Fences, barriers, and enclosures can be an effective means of keeping people out of the water or preventing them from accidentally falling in. However, the height, design, and materials used for construction should all be carefully considered before installation. Although tall security-style fences can make formidable barriers to keep even persistent rule breakers from entering the water, they may also prevent access for maintenance to the areas they surround, impede emergency crews, interfere with the natural movements of wildlife, and negatively diminish an otherwise serene view of the water. Furthermore, they are difficult and time consuming to install, remove, and reinstall, which may make them impractical for seasonal or temporary applications. Other than for use around marinas and boatyards and in storage facilities where other security concerns exist, this type of enclosure is limited for waterfront and marine applications.

Shorter fences, rails, or barriers are more commonly used in waterfront areas with the goal of preventing people from accidentally entering the water or creating a visual border that suggests people not go beyond it. However, there are still several site- and goal-specific considerations that should be discussed before selecting a particular type of fence or barrier. For example, in areas where there is concern over small children and pets getting in the water, a short solid fence may be preferable to a railing that children and pets could easily get under. Similarly, although wooden and plastic snow fences may be an effective means of temporarily keeping people out of the water on lakes and ponds, they are certainly not likely to stand up to wave action or to flood conditions. When choosing the proper fence, barrier, or enclosure for a shorefront area, questions should focus on site attributes such as permanent, temporary, or seasonal installation; exposure to the elements (sun, salt, sand, wind, rain); user characteristics such as age and activity preferences; and the actual goals of installing the device (safety, security, access). Once these

questions are answered, agency personnel can better choose the fence or barrier height, design, and materials that will best meet their needs from the many available alternatives.

Making Changes to the Physical Environment

Although white sandy beaches leading to gradually deepening water are extremely inviting to swimmers and waders, other shoreline features can often discourage the use of our waterways. Several shoreline features can be altered to make waterways, particularly lakes and rivers, less accommodating and accessible to the public for swimming.

Wetlands Restoration

In addition to the positive environmental benefits of wetlands restoration along river and lake banks, these wetlands (swamps and marshes) are not attractive areas for recreational swimming. For the most part, they are too shallow or have too inconsistent a depth to allow for any sustained swimming, and since they are rich in plant life both alive and drowned, they are often very difficult to navigate. Furthermore, as part of their environmental benefits, they provide great habitats for many species of wildlife perceived to be harmful or scary to the general public. An added benefit of restoring wetlands is that although swimming access has been limited, recreation opportunities for wildlife viewing and walking may be increased through the construction of raised boardwalk trails where people can enjoy the proximity to water and wetlands while staying safe and dry above the water.

Bulkheads

Bulkheads and seawalls can discourage potential swimmers and waders from entering the water because they eliminate what is often a gradual slope toward the water and replace it with a sudden drop-off. Furthermore, it is often difficult to accurately assess water depth without this gradual slope. Many people are intimidated by these sheer drops from land to water and the fact that they are unable to test the depth slowly and gradually. Although this type of shoreline modification is valuable in reducing temptations to enter the water, it can also create a severe hazard from people falling over the sides into water of an indeterminate depth and potentially create a situation where it is very difficult to get out of the water and onto safe ground. With this in mind, it is recommended that bulkheads always be accompanied by a safety rail or fence designed to prevent people from accidentally falling or wandering off the edge. "No diving" and "no jumping" signs may also be needed on bulkheads because they may be a temptation for some daredevils. An additional advantage of bulkheads is that they are proven erosion control devices.

Riprap

Riprap is fist- to head-size rocks that are poured over a moderate grade on the shores of lakes and rivers. Like bulkheads, riprap is an excellent erosion control device. However, unlike bulkheads, it is generally used as a portion of a gradual slope rather than to create a drop-off or wall as a grade separation. Although riprap is normally found on areas such as the water sides of earthen dams and other areas that are susceptible to erosion, there is no reason why it cannot be incorporated at any portion of a river or lakeshore. The reason riprap can be an effective method to control water access is that it is difficult and cumbersome to travel over on foot, particularly with bare feet. The rocks that make up the riprap are often unstable and are of a size that makes them extremely uncomfortable to walk over. A final advantage of riprap is that compared with a bulkhead or seawall, it is fairly inexpensive to install and can be done with little planning and labor.

Enforcing Rules

Perhaps the most effective way to keep people from swimming and wading is through the use of sensible, well-publicized rules and subsequent enforcement of these rules. However, for this to be most effective, two items should be in place:

The riprap pictured here not only protects the stone wall and sidewalk but also keeps pedestrians from getting swept into the sea.

1. **Realistic and enforceable rules.** Making rules for the sake of having rules is never a good idea. Furthermore, rules are most effective when there is little ambiguity in their interpretation. For example, it is easy to enforce as well as comply with the regulation "No swimming or wading." If we are going to go to the trouble of enforcing rules, then we need to make sure people are aware of them and able to comply with them and that the rules are easily enforceable.

2. **Perceived presence of authority.** For the public to take rules and regulations seriously, they need to perceive that there is legitimate authority to enforce the rules and that there are consequences for noncompliance. Merely posting rules on a sign and having no patrols present is similar to posting a speed limit on a highway without patrolling it. Although some people will adhere to the posted speed limit, the majority of the public will exceed it if they perceive there is no chance of it's being enforced. Additionally, personnel who enforce rules should have legitimate authority to do so and should be appropriately trained in both law enforcement and public relations. Would-be enforcers who either lack legitimate authority or are too eager to issue citations result in willful noncompliance with regulations, poor public perceptions, or both.

Overall Considerations

The preceding section of this chapter offers several methods for keeping the public out of the water at nonswimming beaches and waterfront areas. Although all these methods have merits, not all of them are equally effective in all situations. Since each beach and waterfront area is unique and may also have specific goals and objectives related to its use, several factors should be considered when choosing from these or other potential methods not included in this chapter:

- Initial cost: What is the total cost of implementing the method? Consider materials, construction, planning and design, and installation labor costs.
- Likelihood of achieving objectives: What are the exact objectives of the effort to keep people out of the water? User and site characteristics as well as previous problems and seasonal or temporary versus permanent closures should all be considered here.
- Aesthetic considerations: What impact on available views and overall aesthetics of the facility will the method have? How will it affect the enjoyment and satisfaction of beach and waterfront users? The overall impacts should be considered and placed in context with agency objectives.
- Long-term labor cost: What are the annual and long-term costs associated with the method? Annual preventive, routine, and repair maintenance for the method should be determined as well as increases in labor associated with monitoring, inspecting, and rule enforcement should all be considered.

Essentially, the process of choosing and implementing a method comes down to a cost–benefit analysis that compares the potential of each alternative method of meeting agency goals and objectives with the long-term costs associated with implementing the method. Note that aesthetic effects can be thought of as either a benefit if the project provides new opportunities or improves the look of a facility or as a cost if the project will have a negative effect on user experiences. Appendix A provides a matrix that can be used to help individuals or agencies choose which method will work best for their own situations. None of the methods included in this chapter needs to be the sole method employed to keep people out of the water. In many cases, a combination of these tools will be most effective.

Summary

Regardless of why you want to keep people out of the water, or the methods you choose to do so, you need to keep beach and waterfront areas pleasant and inviting for the public in general. By incorporating the methods outlined in this chapter with well-maintained waterfront and shore areas that provide alternatives to swimming such as playgrounds, picnic areas, walking and biking trails, and wildlife viewing areas, you can ensure that your visitors will leave your shores both dry and satisfied. Remember that a view of the water is more important to some people than getting into or on the water.

Swimming Beach Safety

Providing safe and enjoyable open-water areas should be the goal of all beach managers and those managing waterfronts. Aesthetics and attractions must be balanced with safety at all open-water areas in order to maximize safe use. Safety and enjoyment of beaches can and should coexist; they do not have to be mutually exclusive.

Open water has a multitude of benefits for beachgoers. But open water has risks, even more than swimming pools and water parks, because of ever-changing natural environmental factors.

Environmental Considerations

When planning to place and design a beach, it is both possible and desirable to plan around environmental factors such as the sun and wind. When a beach occurs naturally rather than being designed, planned, and constructed, considering environmental factors is still important, but too often there is not much that can be done about them.

Orientation

Although maximum sun exposure is desirable, western exposure can make supervision difficult. When a setting sun is in the line of sight of a lifeguard or parent providing visual surveillance, changing position and line of sight to avoid the direct rays of the sun is of ultimate importance. Placing the beach upstream of pollution and in areas protected from the wind also makes for a safer and more enjoyable beach.

From a water safety perspective, the sun can be extremely detrimental. Glare from the sun can hide distressed swimmers from the most vigilant of lifeguards. Hats, polarized sunglasses, and binoculars may be helpful when lifeguards must look toward the sun as they supervise patrons. Also, whenever possible, lifeguards should position themselves with their backs to the sun. This may require lifeguards to guard from the water and visually scan in toward the beach. This of course would be difficult to accomplish when the sun is setting over the Pacific Ocean.

Wind

As a general rule of thumb, windy beaches do not make good swimming beaches. Strong winds usually produce big waves and strong currents, both of which can be menacing toward swimmers. Tourists typically do not appreciate this simple yet important water safety fact. Beaches with strong winds are better suited for surfing, windsurfing, kiteboarding, and other aquatic activities. Swimming and other aquatic sports requiring the wind should be segregated for safety. Whenever possible, swimming beaches should be selected for their lack of wind. When planning a safe swimming beach, consider the leeward side of land masses and coves.

Waves and Currents

Waves and currents tend to go hand in hand. Although they can produce fun-filled days for strong swimmers, they can be deadly for weaker swimmers. Many lifeguarding associations and agencies have rating systems for waves and currents. Flags and signs are often used in combination to educate and warn beachgoers, especially tourists. Every attempt should be made to place safe swimming beaches in areas with calmer waters; when this is not possible, aggressive warnings are highly recommended. As the height and strength of waves increase, so do the currents, especially rip currents. Rip currents are the number one hazard at surf beaches.

Turbidity

Turbidity refers to the lack of water clarity (visibility) created by suspended particles and particulate matter. Clear water is greatly preferred for safe swimming. Turbid water may be clean water, but beachgoers prefer clear water, often assuming that clear water is clean. Clear water can be polluted, however. Most open-water beaches are subjected to turbidity problems as environmental conditions change. Only swimming pools and water parks can maintain clear water through effective water chemistry and efficient filtration. Hence, water turbidity remains one of the inherent dangers at open-water beaches. As weather and water conditions change to produce turbidity, supervision should be increased to prevent someone from slipping below the surface unseen.

Water clarity standards for beaches can often be unrealistic and impractical. Although it is true that clear water tends to be safer (not necessarily cleaner), in many cases it is too difficult to prevent turbidity at open-water beaches. Some confined flat-water beaches determine clarity by means of a black and white disc on a measured line. Good visibility might be established at 4 feet (1.2 m), which would then translate to a beach day with full capacity allowed in the swimming area. On days with only 2 feet (.6 m) visibility, the beach capacity might be cut to allow only half the normal full capacity in the designated swimming area.

This outflow pipe is an example of a man-made hazard. The exposed pilings, which prevent the pipe from moving, are exposed at low tide but hidden at high tide.

Temperature

Ideal water temperatures range between 70 and 80 degrees Fahrenheit (21 to 27 °C). Water temperatures above 85 degrees Fahrenheit (29 °C) and below 65 degrees Fahrenheit (18 °C) can be harmful to both swimmers and waders. Air temperature should also be considered for safe swimming in the open water. When it comes to temperature, the 120-degree rule should apply. When the air temperature plus the water temperature combined is less than 120 degrees Fahrenheit (49 °C), it's too cold to swim (Scheder 2010).

Slope

The bottom or floor of the designated swimming or wading area should slope gently and uniformly toward deeper water. In designated swimming areas where the slope becomes more noticeable, it is even more important that the bottom be uniform and free of underwater obstructions such as weeds, structures, stumps, holes, and drop-offs. These unexpected underwater hazards pose an immediate threat to swimmers and waders alike.

Drop-offs and holes are especially dangerous for waders and nonswimmers, who can suddenly find themselves in water over their heads. A gradual, uniform, and consistent slope is imperative to ensure safety.

In shallow-water areas, it is best for the slope to remain between 2 and 5 percent. In deep-water areas, the slope may increase up to 10 percent, but remember that deep-water areas must be closely monitored and reserved for swimmers only. Some swimming areas have solved the slope and bottom material issues by drawing down lakes and actually paving the bottom with concrete. This action illustrates just how important the slope and bottom material is for water safety. It is important to understand that at surf beaches, as the slope increases, so does the severity of plunging waves and shorebreak.

Water Circulation

To maintain good water quality that ensures swimmer health and safety, it is important to have good water flow and circulation through the swimming area without excessive currents. Whenever practical and possible, a constant flow of clean, fresh water should move through the swimming area to displace older, dirtier water. Ideally, the beach should be placed in such a locale that this occurs naturally. Particularly for smaller impoundments of water found in freshwater lakes and ponds, it would be wise to consider adding fresh water to the designated swimming area through water fountains such as raindrops or mushrooms. The source of water in these cases can be located in a cleaner portion of the lake, or wells can even be drilled for this purpose. Aerators do not necessarily move new water into a swimming area but can be used effectively to oxygenate the water and create circulation that moves bad water out.

Beach Material

Sand is often considered the only suitable material for a swimming beach, but that is just not true. Around the world, some very safe and aesthetically pleasing beaches are composed of other materials underfoot such as stone, pebbles, seashells, volcanic lava, and grass. Beach sand comes from a variety of sources. The most common type of beach sand in the United States is made up of lightly colored quartz or feldspar grains produced from the erosion of weathering rocks, cliffs, and bottom materials at the beach. Some beaches, particularly those located in the tropics, are composed mostly of crushed seashells and corals. Still others can be made of volcanic rock or lava. Beach material, regardless of what it is made of, is constantly on the move, either migrating toward and into the water or being moved inland or up and down the beach.

Erosion is a significant problem for those who live and work near a beach and for tourists as well, but beach renourishment projects that may save beaches in the short term come with a host of complicating factors. Such projects are extremely expensive and provide only short-term benefits. Dredging conducted to replenish beach sand can create environmental problems and drastically change the nearshore current system. Not all beaches are appropriate for sand renourishment projects; some beaches may keep their replenished sand for decades, while others may lose much of their replenished sand after the first major storm. Although wide, sandy beaches can mean millions to a local beach economy, sound research must be conducted first to ascertain the

pros and cons of beach renourishment projects. Sand at many beaches can actually be recycled by moving it away from boat ramps and channels and replacing it on the beach where it is better appreciated.

Bottom Material

Firm, stable, uniform bottom material is important. Sand, pea gravel, smooth stones, and even concrete can produce safe and acceptable bottom material. When swimming area bottoms consist of mud or silt, slippage is always a possibility, and a turbidity problem often results. Sand and other bottom materials should be approximately 6 to 12 inches (15 to 30 cm) deep throughout the entire swimming area. Draining down the swimming areas and placing landscaping fabric or PVC membranes over the bottom and then adding 6 to 12 inches of sand or gravel on top of the material works well to cover the mud and silt; it also keeps vegetation to a minimum and even helps water clarity. Above all, sudden holes and drop-offs should be filled in or otherwise eliminated or else the swimming area should be moved.

Safe Site Selection for Unguarded Beaches

Ideally, only the safest beach areas should be selected as unguarded. Beaches that have a subtle slope (3 to 5 percent) and a firm, constant bottom and that are free of vegetation, strong currents, big waves, strong prevailing winds, rocky shorelines, heavy boat traffic, and dangerous marine life are more suitable to be unguarded. But just because some beaches appear to be safer does not mean safety precautions are unnecessary.

Designated Swimming Areas

Careful consideration must be given to choosing and marking designated swimming areas. All swimmers should be directed to a clearly marked, defined, and designated safe swimming area free of surface and underwater hazards that may not be obvious and may go undetected by swimmers and waders alike. Swimmers should be encouraged to stay out of water that has not been designated safe for swimming.

This pretty, calm, and relatively safe pocket beach in San Juan, Puerto Rico, was created by placing several bulkheads and jetties in the mouth of the cove to protect the beach from the raging, and at times dangerous, ocean waves and currents.

Whether deep or shallow, well-designed designated swimming areas provide a significant margin of safety. Internationally, studies reveal that nearly 75 percent of all drownings occur outside designated swimming areas. Additionally, rescue and resuscitation efforts outside designated swimming areas are only 35 percent effective compared with 75 to 95 percent effective inside. A 10-year study conducted by the Army Corps of Engineers clearly revealed that well-designed and clearly designated swimming areas can and will significantly reduce drowning deaths:

> Between 1971 and 1987 there were approximately 330 drownings per year in Army Corps of Engineer aquatic facilities. After the new swimming beach design criteria were introduced . . . , drownings were reduced to 183 drownings a year between 1988 and 1998. It is important to note that these reductions in drowning were accomplished without lifeguards on duty. Historically, the Army Corps of Engineers have provided water safety through warnings and education, not with lifeguards. (Keshler 1999)

This information sends a clear message: Beachgoers should be aggressively educated to swim in designated safe swimming areas and encouraged to stay out of the water in unsafe, undesignated swimming areas. Proactive prevention campaigns such as this can be best accomplished with a combination of effective safety signage and safety patrols.

Buoyant Lines and Depth Markings

To promote safety, the safe swimming area should be clearly defined with buoyant lines, buoys, and depth markers whenever possible. For surf beaches, this may be particularly difficult, if not impossible in some cases. Water depth is an important consideration whenever planning, designing, or placing a beach. A maximum depth of 4.5 to 5 feet (1.4 to 1.5 m) is more than sufficient for most beaches. It is also important when practical to clearly mark and illustrate the depth so that swimmers can see the depth markings from the waterline. This may be accomplished with buoys and depth-gauge poles. A topographical map of the swimming area with depths noted is also a good idea.

Buoying off separate sections at 2.5 feet (.8 m), 3.5 feet (1.1 m), and 4.5 feet (1.4 m) provides extra layers of protection for preventing young non-swimmers from entering water over their heads. The buoyant lines themselves are important for drowning prevention. Simply stringing lines that are loose and slightly buoyant across a swimming area is not adequate. Designated swimming areas need brightly colored, tightly strung, and very buoyant lines to not only clearly delineate the safe swimming and wading areas but also to provide buoyancy when weaker swimmers need it. Larger buoys in the corners of the swimming and wading areas also help better define the designated safe areas. A lap lane with a depth of 5 feet (1.5 m) of water just for serious swimmers may offer the best margin of safety.

Deep-Water Areas

Deep-water areas are not recommended for unguarded beaches. When water depths are greater than 5 feet (1.5 m), it becomes significantly more difficult to rescue, recover, and resuscitate victims. This is true even when lifeguards are on duty. Although many flat-water beaches have rafts, diving boards, slides, and other deep-water amenities, these attractions draw weak swimmers and strong swimmers alike. Even when lifeguards are on duty, assisting those in need in water over their heads is extremely difficult. Without lifeguards on duty, rescue of swimmers in deep water is almost impossible. Therefore, deep-water amenities are not recommended for unguarded beaches.

Although deep-water areas were extremely popular in the 1960s, 1970s, and 1980s, their popularity has diminished in recent years, likely because of drownings and litigation that has resulted from deep-water swimming. Competent swimmers have little if any trouble swimming in deep-water areas. The problem has been and continues to be the lack of supervision in these areas and the ease of access to deep water many weaker swimmers have. Just as peer pressure by stronger downhill skiers pulls novice skiers to steep slopes they cannot handle, weaker swimmers are often lured out to deeper water by friends and family who are stronger swimmers. Deep-water rafts and docks with diving boards and slides are a lot of fun and can be very attractive, but they require both supervision and entry requirements. A lack of control and supervision in deep-water areas can quickly lead to drowning.

Open-water areas with depth tend to be deeper and darker than deep-water areas in swimming pools and water parks. As a result, rescue and recovery of near-drowning victims becomes arduous, requiring more time and effort. The risks are especially high in water with limited or poor clarity. Whenever possible, deep-water swimming areas should be maintained only where they are appropriate: good water clarity, consistent depth and bottom conditions, vigilant supervision with deep-water rescue equipment (mask, fins, snorkels), and proactive safety strategies when deep-water swimming areas are open to the public. Beach managers considering deep-water swimming areas should keep in mind that most of the beachgoing public prefer lots of shallow water.

Buffer Zones

Whenever possible, confined beaches with designated swimming areas should have buffer zones—neutral areas to reduce hazardous conflicts between swimmers or waders and other user groups, particularly people using any type of watercraft or specialized equipment. It is preferable to use brightly colored buoys and lines or similar floating objects so that the buffer zone between the designated swimming area and other user areas can be seen from a distance. International "boats keep out" buoys are perhaps the best devices to warn others of swimming and wading areas. These buoys float vertically in the water and utilize a highly visible fluorescent orange diamond. It is best to place these buoys 500 to 1,000 feet (150 to 300 m) outside the swimming area and approximately 200 feet (60 m) apart. At the very least, these warning buoys should be placed at the corners of the designated swim area. Buoy placement is always a problem at surf beaches and other water areas with strong currents.

River Swimming Beaches

River beaches tend to have longer designated swimming areas along the river banks. They also tend to be more narrow (i.e., not out into the river, where stronger currents and deeper water is usually found). When river beaches are planned, river traffic must also be considered. Faster and larger boats creating unexpected waves in the designated swimming area can be especially troublesome. With proper planning, design, operation, and management river beaches can be safe and enjoyable.

Designated Wading (Nonswimming) Areas

Especially at American beaches, most beachgoers walk and play in the shallow water rather than swim. For this reason, shallow-water wading areas should also be designated within or adjacent to the larger, more generic designated swimming area.

Buoyed Lines and Depth Markings

It is important to segregate the shallow-water area for nonswimmers and waders from the deeper designated swimming area to prevent younger nonswimmers from accidentally getting into water over their heads. Buoyant lines on the surface help keep young children in the safe confines of the wading areas. Some flat-water beaches have even placed in-water fencing below or just outside the buoyant lines to better safeguard youngsters. This is especially important if deep water can be accessed in close proximity to the designated shallow-water wading area. Inexpensive snow fencing has worked well in this application. Surf beaches typically cannot designate a wading area; whenever possible, a nearby bay or sound with safe shallow water without waves and currents should be selected and promoted for nonswimmers. The depth of the water should be clearly identified whenever possible.

Wading Area Depth

Shallow-water wading areas must offer safe surroundings, and the maximum water depth should not exceed 3 feet (.9 m). A uniform and constant bottom free of holes and drop-offs is extremely important.

Support Features and Facilities

Some beaches do an admirable job of combining several different amenities in the same central location. Fort Lauderdale, Florida, combines playgrounds, shaded picnic areas, and activity areas for basketball, volleyball, and beach tennis all directly on the soft, sandy beach. This combined activity area is located between the parking lot and the surf beach, has bathrooms and showers, and is accessible for people with disabilities.

Entrance Station

Whenever a fee is charged to access the beach or when access is made through one entry point, an enhanced entrance area is a good idea. A beach entrance station is an important facility because this is where the beachgoers get their first impression of the beach. Rules, regulations, water safety information, directions, emergency contacts and information, weather forecasts, and water and air temperatures can be posted at this prime location. When other constructed facilities are limited at the beach, the first aid station can be maintained at the entrance station, provided it is not too far from the beach. Likewise, lost and found items may be located here so that those leaving the beach can check for the items on their way out. If fees are collected, the beach entrance location should be secure. The entrance station should not be considered a toll booth simply to collect fees, however. It should be a welcoming information center where each and every guest is greeted, educated, and warned of the hazards existing at the beach. Perhaps this is the best place to disseminate the most pertinent information to guests because this may be their only stop before entering the water. Make sure the safety of all guests is the message conveyed when people first pass through the entrance station.

Although the entrance station can perform a variety of vitally important functions, the facility should be designed and operated to allow guests to pass through in an efficient manner. In addition to the building required for the entrance station, ancillary structures such as parking for employees and guests, restrooms, pay phones, and information kiosks (maps, brochures, emergency information) are necessary. Further, the best-equipped entrance station in the world will not be as valuable if the wrong employees are working there. Friendly and outgoing employees are a must. In summary, although entrance stations at the beach need not be as large as welcoming centers on interstate highways, the concept should be the same.

Parking Lots

Because no one enjoys hunting for a place to park, one way swimming beaches limit the number of swimmers on hot weekends is by reducing the number of parking spots available. Particularly when beaches are relatively close to highly populated areas, the larger the parking lot, the more guests will travel to the beach. So when peak attendance is anticipated, such as the Fourth of July weekend, temporarily reducing the size of the parking lot may be an effective water safety strategy. Because each motor vehicle requires 300 square feet (28 sq m), the largest surface area requirement for any beach is usually the parking lot. If a fee is charged for using the beach, charging by the vehicle rather than by the guest is one way of encouraging car pooling and getting by with a smaller parking lot.

Parking lots should be located less than 1,000 feet (300 m) from the entrance to the beach. When the lot is more than 1,000 feet away, drop-off points are strongly encouraged. For remote parking lots, shuttle buses or trams are a good idea to provide transportation to the beach. Although beachgoers love to pull right up to the back edge of the beach and set up their beach equipment a short walk in front of their cars, this user-friendly option does not lend itself well to educating and warning guests. Whenever possible, visitors leaving their cars for the beach should be channeled through a few entrance points where important safety information can be provided. Visual screening, earth mounding, and landscaping can be used to help hide beach parking lots.

Bathhouses

Bathhouses that include toilets with partitions, sinks and hand dryers, shower stalls, changing areas, and lockers for street clothes and valuables are quickly becoming a thing of the past. Full-service bathhouses are not nearly as important today as they were years ago when entire families changed from elaborate street, work, or church clothes into bathing suits. Rather, many of today's beachgoers swim in the same apparel they arrived in. When bathhouses are available, it is speculated that far less than 10 percent of the beachgoers today actually use them (Griffiths 1999). When municipalities ban changing clothes in public, then bathhouses may be required.

When bathhouses are constructed at a beach, all floors should slope well to drains. The floors must be made of a nonslip material that is also easy to clean. Brushed concrete is a popular bathhouse floor treatment that is relatively inexpensive to install and certainly nonslip, but it is far from being aesthetically appealing. Carpets are never a good idea in any aquatic facility bathhouse or locker room because they harbor moisture, funguses, mold, mildew, and other undesirables. Nonslip runners are often used in locker rooms and bathhouses, but they must be cleaned daily and hung up to dry each evening.

Perhaps the greatest need today is simply toilets and outdoor showers. These two commodities seem to be the most valuable and well used and don't require a structure to contain them. Sinks, counters, and hand dryers can all be located between and outside the men's and women's bathrooms, thus saving both space and money. Unisex family changing rooms and rooms specifically for infant care are important growing trends.

Toilet facilities should be a higher priority than bathhouses. When running water for hand washing is either unavailable or too expensive to install, hand dispensers for liquid antibacterial soaps are highly recommended. It is best to have all toilets located close to the beach. Ideally they should be between 250 and 500 feet (75 to 150 m) from the beach if they cannot be placed directly on the back edge of the beach. When toilets are located more than 500 feet from the beach, there is a good chance the designated swimming area will be used as a toilet.

Showers and Foot-Washing Facilities

Particularly in warm-weather areas, showers and foot-washing facilities are popular and can be located outside, right on the beach and preferably close to the parking lots. Placing the showers and foot-washing stations at the established entrances and exits to the beach also helps to keep sand out of clothes and vehicles. Fortunately, showers and foot-washing stations can be easily accommodated on the same pole, saving both space and money. They are particularly appreciated at saltwater beaches where hair and skin become sticky after swimming. The trend with these showering appliances is to keep them outside rather than inside.

Concession Stands

When it comes to selling food and drink and offering rentals at a beach, one of the first considerations should be who will run the concessions. Either the beach owner or operator can run the food and beverage concession, or bids can be taken from potential vendors. If the owner or operator of the beach elects to run the concession stands, although there is potential for generating more income, it can create significantly more work and stress for the owner or operator. Contracting vendors results in less profit, but this arrangement tends to be much easier and less stressful. Independent contractors can provide a valuable service and at the same time take on the burden, cost, and liability of food and beverage service. Of course the best of both worlds can be achieved when beach management already has someone on staff with a food and beverage or hospitality service background who can run the concession stands.

Regardless of how large or small the concession area is, it should be in close proximity to the beach, with a good view of the water. Recycling and trash receptacles should be in great abundance and emptied regularly. Recycling programs at the beach are especially important, not only because they are environmentally correct but also because they significantly reduce trash on the beach. Aluminum and plastic containers are greatly preferred over glass because of the incompatibility of broken glass and bare feet. Drinking straws and toothpicks are particularly difficult to clean from the beach, and plastic beverage rings endanger fish, birds, and small mammals.

There are numerous benefits in having the concession area centrally located near other amenities such as bathrooms, the first aid room, and the information center. Portable trailers can always be used when buildings are just not available or too costly. Simple pushcarts also tend to work well, particularly if a boardwalk or similar pathway is available.

Lifeguard Quarters

The larger the lifeguard staff, the larger the lifeguard quarters required. In Southern California, lifeguard quarters are control central for the

This lifeguard station, maintained by the City of Los Angeles, is not merely functional; it has been beautified as part of the city's Summer of Color campaign. This is part of the largest art project in the United States, which includes 31 miles of beachfront art.

beach and supply many services and equipment. Whether large or small, these structures should at the very least offer a reprieve from the elements and the noise of the beach crowd. Elevated lifeguard quarters with a good view of the water are highly recommended. Since lifeguards require regular breaks from visual surveillance, these quarters may be the best place to accomplish that. Ice machines, refrigerators, radios, TVs, exercise equipment, and appropriate reading material can all be placed in the lifeguard quarters depending on the size of the lifeguard staff and the budget. Sunscreen should be available because lifeguards are exposed to the harmful UV rays of the sun as well.

Sophisticated communication systems, additional rescue equipment, and vehicles can also be located at the lifeguard quarters. Like the entrance station, the lifeguard station can provide information about water safety, weather, emergency services, and directions. Because all aquatic facilities should have first aid stations, perhaps the best place to have first aid equipment and supplies is in the lifeguard quarters, where lifeguards trained in first aid are available. It is quite acceptable for lifeguards getting a break from the sun and visual surveillance to be applying first aid to those beachgoers in need. Before beach managers place any first aid supplies and equipment in the first aid station, local authorities should first approve their purchase and application.

Lawns

As one might expect, spacious lawns at beaches come with advantages and disadvantages. One advantage is that many people, particularly the elderly and the disabled, prefer lawns to sand because they offer a more stable base on which to traverse. Another advantage is that the sandy beach is less likely to become overcrowded when a nicely mowed lawn provides an alternative for sitting and lounging in the sun. Still another advantage is one of aesthetics; a lush green lawn provides a pleasing contrast to the tan beach sand. Conversely, perhaps the biggest disadvantage of having large lawns is their attractiveness to Canada geese. In most cases, the larger the lawn, the more geese it will attract. Many geese deterrents are available, but these tend to simply reduce the problem by temporarily moving the geese to nearby areas. The deterrents do not

totally eliminate the geese or their associated problems. Geese and other beach pests are discussed in chapter 10. Lawns can also attract annoying insects if the turf is not appropriately treated.

Dry Playgrounds

Dry playgrounds (as opposed to spraygrounds) either on or near the beach are an excellent way of increasing both safety and enjoyment. Playgrounds provide parents and children with a safe alternative to swimming as well as reduce the swimmer load in the designated swimming area. Particularly on busy days, the playground may help keep the swimming area from becoming dangerously overcrowded. When a playground is constructed directly on the beach, a soft sandy landing is naturally provided for safety under the play apparatus. Because most children at the beach do not wear shoes, all play equipment should be designed to safely accommodate bare feet. On busy weekends when safety breaks are taken in many designated swimming areas, the playground can offer families safe recreation alternatives. Parents should supervise their children on the playground as closely as when they are in the water. Although the lifeguards get a break during this time, it is a good idea to send a lifeguard to the playground area to offer additional supervision. All playgrounds should be inspected and certified by the National Recreation and Park Association's National Playground Safety Institute.

Spraygrounds and Spray Parks

Many people who go to the beach are actually not that interested in swimming; they simply want to cool off and enjoy the sights and sounds in and around the water. Spraygrounds and spray parks are playgrounds with interactive water features, mostly intended for younger children who cannot swim or simply need a break from the sun or the swimming area. For those families with younger children, spraygrounds and spray parks are a much safer alternative to swimming at the beach because children can play in the water and get cooled off without being at risk. This on-land water play can assist lifeguards by minimizing the number of young nonswimmers in their zones of coverage. It is also another way of washing away unwanted sand before getting in a vehicle to return home.

Picnic Areas

The appropriate placement of picnic areas, particularly for flat-water beaches, is important. Whenever possible, picnic areas should be close to both parking lots and the beach, perhaps even between the two. Having a view of the designated swimming area is also considered ideal. Picnic areas that are not located in close proximity to the parking area require curb-cuts or pull-offs to allow vehicles to stop without creating traffic jams so that guests will not have to carry heavy coolers, grills, and other items long distances. Surveys show that picnickers prefer swimming over other recreation activities, so having ample picnic areas at beaches should be an important consideration. Shade is also important for picnickers, and if an adequate number of trees is not available for shade, then consider constructing picnic shelters. Although picnic areas at flat-water beaches are almost as important as the swimming and wading areas, picnicking directly on the beach at surf and coastal beaches can be especially challenging because of litter and bird control as well as trash removal. Contact other surf beaches for best practices regarding eating and drinking on the beach.

Beach Volleyball Courts

There is no doubt about it, beach volleyball on Southern California beaches is huge. Scores and scores of volleyball nets are permanently placed at the backs of beaches for pickup games and tournaments. Regardless of where a beach is located, beach volleyball should be strongly encouraged because it requires little money, equipment, and space and causes few, if any, injuries or conflicts. Where vandalism is a concern, players can be asked to bring their own nets in addition to their own volleyballs.

On Southern California beaches, bike paths are so busy and so popular that parallel paths are often needed to separate walkers from bikers, roller bladers, and skateboarders.

Other Activity Areas

A variety of play areas and activities can be inexpensively and practically added to existing beaches in order to cater to all ages and visitors. These games and activity areas can add immeasurable pleasure to beachgoers who seek more than just swimming and sunbathing.

Lawn Games

When large lawns are available, a wide range of activities can be offered including volleyball, softball, tetherball, and horseshoes. Boccie is a great beach activity, whether it is played on a lawn or on the beach itself. It requires no special field of play or equipment except the boccie balls. It must be remembered, however, that large lawns attract geese.

Hiking, Biking, and Walking Trails

With the fitness craze for all ages still growing in America, hiking, biking, and walking trails on the back edge of beaches are extremely popular, particularly if a view of the water exists. Joggers, walkers, cyclists, dog walkers, in-line skaters, and skateboarders all gravitate to these beachside trails. As an example of popularity, during March 2009, I simply counted bikers riding past a fixed point on the Strand in Hermosa Beach, California. On average, 25 cyclists rode by every minute. That means in warm weather with extended daylight, between 25,000 and 30,000 cyclists could be using the trail. And this figure does not include other users (walkers, joggers). It appears that bike trails at the beach are a great investment.

Summary

The natural and environmental conditions at a beach can dictate the type of activities that will be available to guests. Knowing the beach characteristics and planning the beach and swimming areas around them makes perfect sense. Offering more than swimming for guests not only adds diversity and enjoyment to the beach experience but can also add a margin of safety by giving safe and restful alternatives to the water, particularly when safety breaks are implemented. Consider the applications in this chapter for a safer, more enjoyable, more memorable beach experience.

Above-Water Structure Safety

Above-water structures such as piers, docks, and jetties can give beachgoers an intimate experience with the water without immersing themselves in it. Visitors can observe wave action, bottom conditions, competing currents, marine life, and more from above-water structures without getting wet or even wearing a bathing suit. In addition, recreation activities such as fishing and crabbing, where appropriate, can be accomplished from above-water structures.

Beachgoers often want a close-up view of the open water without necessarily getting wet. Whenever a pier, dock, or jetty is in place, visitors often access these structures to get a better view of the water and the shoreline behind them. But too often, walking, running, or playing on a pier, dock, or jetty can be risky. During inclement weather, accessing piers, docks, jetties, and breakwaters can be downright dangerous. When people climb up onto these structures, it seems as though they leave their common sense back on the beach. Therefore, when these structures can be accessed from the beach, boardwalk, or parking lot, it is necessary to aggressively educate and warn people that they may be in danger if they venture onto them. If a particular structure is not safe for the public, appropriate signage should be displayed. When the public is allowed to access these structures, layers of protection for piers and docks should be in place and enforced, including effective barriers, signage, and patrols.

Types of Above-Water Structures

A wide variety of artificial structures can be added to waterfronts to enhance the beach experience. Whether you are adding a structure or managing an existing one, some tips are offered here for safety and enhancement. Remember to consult www.ada.gov for the 2010 ADA standards addressing accessibility issues for piers and docks.

Piers and Docks

Although there are many different types of docks and piers, most are intended to get people on and over the water. Whether visitors are mooring boats or fishing, safety should be the rule while increasing accessibility for all.

Groins

Groins are strong structures made of stone, steel, concrete, or even timber that are intended to stop the longshore (parallel) transport of sand up or down the beach. Groins are constructed from the beach into the water through the surf zone in a perpendicular direction. The structures themselves can be an attraction for fishermen and wave jumpers, and it is generally a good idea to ban pedestrians from groins. Although they work fairly well in preventing erosion, in some cases sand can build up on one side of a groin while being lost on the other side. This loss and gain of sand around each groin creates a scalloped beach effect. This makes it difficult to supervise these areas and difficult to maintain the integrity of the beach. In addition, strong currents can be produced directly alongside groins. So although groins initially appear to be a good idea, they can produce some negative and even dangerous effects. Over time, groins placed from the water to the beach for sand control often transform a straight beach into a carved-up beach.

The fabulously famous Santa Monica Pier offers so much more than just a bird's-eye view of the water.

This groin both protects the pipe located within it and keeps people away. Unfortunately, groins such as this also create dangerous currents and obstructions.

Jetties

Jetties are structures placed on the sides of an inlet to keep it open and navigable by preventing the longshore transport of sand into the inlet. They can be made of stone, concrete, steel, or other suitable materials, and they attract a variety of user groups (fishermen, wave jumpers, sightseers). In many cases, these people must be kept off the jetties, or safety equipment such as railings need to be added to the structures. Effective warning signage should also be in place because not only is drowning a possibility after a fall from a jetty but so is getting run over by boats.

Bulkheads and Seawalls

Bulkheads and seawalls are typically made of rigid materials similar to groins and jetties but may be placed either at the back of the beach or in the water. When bulkheads and seawalls are placed behind the beach, their purpose is to protect the beach sand and dunes from erosion through wave attacks and storm-surge flooding. When bulkheads and seawalls are placed out in the water, their purpose is to protect the beach by stopping large waves. Bulkheads and seawalls typically have gaps between them, leading to the possibility of currents rushing through these openings. Although in-water bulkheads do in fact calm the waters close to the beach, they can help create new currents between and around the structures.

Potential Above-Water Structure Hazards

The primary purpose of structures such as piers, breakwaters, and docks is to reduce wave action in order to provide calm water and shelter or mooring for vessels and water enthusiasts. On larger bodies of water such as oceans and the Great Lakes, these structures are designed as navigation tools and often have beacons or lighthouses located on them.

Wind

Recreational use of above-water structures is not safe when they are wet or when it is windy. Unfortunately, the wind generates waves that crash onto and against these structures, which in turn seduce sightseers. Wave jumping is a popular but extremely dangerous activity on piers, docks, and jetties. It brings adventuresome people to piers when waves are crashing over them. Strong swimmers and good athletes have died while attempting to jump over waves crashing across docks and piers. This type of activity must of course be banned. Where pedestrian traffic is unsafe and not allowed on piers and jetties, signs with the following message should be posted: "Structure not designed or intended for public use."

Diving

There are approximately 800 to 900 catastrophic spinal injuries caused by diving into shallow water each year in the United States. Approximately two-thirds of these injuries occur in open-water areas as opposed to swimming pools and water parks (Griffiths 2003).

A significant number of these open-water neck injuries are caused by diving off docks and piers and other similar structures. For some reason, many people believe that the farther into the water a dock or pier extends, the deeper the water will be. This of course is not necessarily true; the depth of water under a dock or pier varies widely with its geographical location. Docks and piers located on the Gulf of Mexico for instance can extend hundreds of yards into the gulf, and the water depth can still be far too shallow for safe diving. A 10-foot (3 m) minimum depth is normally considered safe for diving from a structure into the open water. Unless a dock or pier is specifically designed for safe diving, diving should be aggressively banned from these structures.

Swimming

Swimming around structures such as piers, docks, jetties, and breakwaters can also be extremely dangerous. Dangers include currents created by the structure, obstructions that may cause injuries and entrapment under and around the structure, and the inability to observe and supervise the swimmers under the structure. Unseen hazards just below the waterline include concrete, rocks, pipes, cables, and strong currents and have all directly or indirectly killed swimmers and divers. Swimming should be banned near all unsafe structures.

In addition, surfing under piers and docks can be an exciting sport but is extremely dangerous. Surfing, windsurfing, and other water sport activities should be done far from these structures.

Safety Strategies for Above-Water Structures

When pedestrians are allowed on above-water structures, access should be reserved for good weather only. During inclement weather, pedestrians can fall and slip from piers and docks. They can also be washed off or blown off these structures.

- Railings or fencing is a welcome safety feature.
- Signs and warnings should be conspicuously placed on both the horizontal planks and the vertical pilings. When wooden planks are used for the horizontal surface of these structures, carving the letters into the boards and painting the letters in bright colors will be both effective and vandal proof. Perhaps the most important warnings for piers, docks, jetties, and breakwaters are as follows:

  No swimming.

  No diving.

  No running.

  Slippery when wet.

- Posting rules and regulations for which activities are permitted and which are not is also a good idea. Rules and regulations must not take priority over the warning signs just mentioned.
- Rescue equipment should be kept on piers and docks. Ring buoys are popular and practical. Where theft is common, placing ring buoys behind glass is a good idea. These emergency boxes can also send out an alert when the window is broken. Call boxes reserved exclusively for emergencies are also helpful.

Hermosa Beach, California, implemented a strong yet attractive protective railing system with appropriate warnings.

- Nonslip surfaces are extremely important for structures and surfaces that are often wet.

Particularly for adolescents and young adults, above-water structures like piers, docks, bulkheads, and jetties are often an invitation to dive and swim even though they are not intended for those activities. If not signed and protected well, above-water structures can become an attractive nuisance that may lead to serious accidents.

Summary

With all structures that extend into the water, prevention is the key to averting accidents and saving lives. Rescues and resuscitations around these structures, particularly during inclement weather, may not be realistic, so proactive prevention programs are a must. Check the references for a pier safety video and brochure put out by the Grand Haven, Michigan, Pier Safety Task Force.

9

Operational Considerations and Safety Strategies

The devil is in the details. Running a beach is more comprehensive than simply opening in the morning and closing at night. Many policies, procedures, and practices should be evaluated before, during, and after the season. Consider this to be a "spring cleaning" chapter, where you reevaluate what you are doing at the waterfront and why. Assess areas of operations that you can either improve or eliminate.

When it comes to operating a beach, many questions must first be answered. Will the beach be free to the public, or will a fee be charged? Will there be lifeguards on duty, or will visitors swim at their own risk? Will the beach remain in its natural state, affected by environmental and human factors, or will the beach be maintained by humans or machines? Will the beach be open all the time, or will there be times during daylight hours in which it is closed? And what about pets, nudists, smoking, glass, alcohol, ball playing, and other considerations? All these questions are significant, and they will certainly affect safety and enjoyment at the beach. Following are some policy decisions you will need to consider.

Policy Decisions Affecting Safety and Beach Operations

Know the strengths and weaknesses of the beach along with the types of activities offered and the people visiting the beach. This chapter is about transitioning policies and procedures into practice.

Swimming Hours

An important consideration that merits serious discussion is whether the beach will be continuously open to the public or whether there will be restricted hours during which the public can use the beach. Many coastal areas around the world allow their beaches to be accessible to the public 24 hours a day, seven days a week. But many other beaches, especially smaller, inland beaches, restrict their hours of operation. Particularly when it comes to swimming, if the hours are restricted at the beach, they should be clearly and conspicuously posted. If the hours of operation are restricted (e.g., 11:00 a.m. to 7:00 p.m.), will those hours be enforced, and if so, how? Although fining people for swimming while the beach is closed may seem like an effective way of keeping people out of the water, it requires significant amounts of time, money, and personnel that can be better spent elsewhere in the community. The trend of late has been to discourage swimming outside the designated swimming area and when there are

no lifeguards on duty. Hence, the concept of "swim at your own risk" is utilized before and after hours.

Guarded Versus Unguarded Beaches

Although it is believed by most professionals that lifeguards are the best option when it comes to protecting patrons, it is difficult, if not impossible, to guard all bodies of water with qualified lifeguards. In addition, some water safety experts believe that when lifeguards are on duty, parents become complacent and do not attend to their children in the water as vigilantly. When the decision is made to have lifeguards, an entire progression of additional requirements commences. Particularly in municipalities that do not require lifeguards, when lifeguards are placed on duty because it is believed to be the right thing to do, the bar of liability is significantly raised. When it comes to lifeguarding beaches, we should do it right or not at all. Today, the standard of care required when lifeguards are on duty is significantly higher than it was just 10 years ago. The United States Lifesaving Association is a wonderful reference, resource, role model, and training agency for open-water lifeguards. See chapter 12 for more information about the USLA.

Although lifeguards are arguably the best means of maintaining safe and enjoyable beaches, the plain fact is lifeguards may not be available at all beaches. When lifeguards are not available, parents tend to watch their children more diligently, and weaker swimmers may behave more reasonably. On beaches where lifeguards are not required, aggressive education and warning programs must be in place to safeguard beachgoers. Most important, notice of and directions to the nearest guarded beaches is recommended in the same fashion that we direct people with disabilities to more accessible beaches.

Families with younger children should be strongly encouraged to go to guarded beaches only. Rural and rustic beaches often are not expected to have lifeguards. Additionally, at beaches where parking is lacking along with restrooms and central entrances, lifeguards are not usually anticipated. When swimming is permitted at these beaches and the "swim at your own risk" concept is utilized, more aggressive signs are recommended such as those described in chapter 5.

Lifejackets and Other Flotation Devices

Perhaps one of the most controversial issues in water safety today, whether at pools, water parks, or beaches, is the use of flotation devices. A strong trend in the United States is to allow only U.S. Coast Guard–approved type III lifejackets. Although no flotation device is perfect, type III personal flotation devices (PFDs) are comfortable to wear and tend to keep the body vertical in the water, with the head above the surface. These PFDs will not deflate or slip off, provided of course that they are properly fitted. Nonswimmers wearing PFDs must still be closely supervised.

Loaner Lifejackets

Loaner lifejackets come highly recommended for the most popular and frequented beach access points. Providing free lifejackets is common in the water park industry, where employees can monitor park gates to help control loss from theft. Lifejackets hung on a Peg-Board with brief safety messages work on many waterfronts and campgrounds around the world. The lifejackets should be returned to the board when no longer in use. To minimize loss from theft, "Property of . . ." should be boldly imprinted on each lifejacket. The lifejackets should be put out in the morning and secured each night to prevent loss. Local, state, or national companies may wish to donate to or sponsor the loaner lifejacket program.

When worn and appropriately fitted, lifejackets do save lives. Unfortunately, many children of tender years are not actively supervised around the water. Parents are frequently seen more than an arm's distance away from their children, reading, or even sleeping on the beach while their children play at water's edge. Lifeguards report having rescued children floating facedown right next to parents who were talking to friends and family members, oblivious to the child's distress. Lifejackets provide an additional layer of protection and enhance safety at waterfront areas.

Flotation Toys

Although there are numerous inexpensive flotation toys on the market, all are ineffective as life preservers, and many are not safe to use and can actually promote inadequate supervision of children and drowning. Flotation toys typically come in two different forms: inflatables and noninflatables. The most popular noninflatable at this time is undoubtedly the noodle. Very inexpensive and easy to use, this Styrofoam tube can be used for water exercise and even for rescue as an extension device. But when it comes to nonswimmers, the noodle provides buoyancy only when the tube is being held by hand or placed under the arms. Noodles can be safely and enjoyably used by adult swimmers but should never be used by nonswimmers, especially young children, as a buoyancy device. Young, nonswimming children have used noodles to access deeper water and have drowned when they slipped off while being inadequately supervised.

Water wings, or floogles, are another popular flotation device. When properly inflated and fitted on the upper arms, water wings can be used safely and effectively only when an adult supervisor is within arm's reach. The major criticism of water wings is that they can deflate or slip off the child's arm. This leads to a quick loss of buoyancy and a life-threatening situation. Particularly in open water that is not crystal clear, a nonswimming child can quickly submerge and not be found in a timely fashion, with catastrophic results.

Lightweight plastic rafts can also pose problems. Especially when offshore breezes blow

The award-winning loaner lifejacket program is one of many recent improvements at Lake Elsinore, California.

the rafts into deeper water, those attempting to recover them have been known to fatigue, panic, and drown quickly.

A strong and clear flotation device policy must be established and signed aggressively. Because beaches compete with pools and water parks for patrons, when a total ban is placed on all flotation devices, attendance may suffer. A delicate balance needs to be maintained between safety and enjoyment. When certain forms of buoyancy toys are banned, it is best to alert guests *before* they remove them from their vehicles and drag them to the beach. This will help minimize customer conflicts.

Floating Attractions

With the growing popularity of water parks and family aquatic centers, some flat-water beaches may see the need to add floating attractions to their waterfronts to compete for patronage. Adding floating attractions such as inflatable slides, obstacle courses, icebergs, blobs, and trampolines should certainly make flat-water beaches more attractive to many. Although these water features are exciting and fun, they do result in a wide variety of injuries. One of the advantages of these oversized toys is that they can be removed from the water temporarily, depending on the situation.

To use floating attractions in the safest manner possible, deep water must be present under the entire length of the attraction, and no one should be allowed to play or swim in the water below. In some cases, floating water features are placed in shallow-water areas. When this occurs, all headfirst entries including diving must be totally banned.

When recommended by a manufacturer, height and weight restrictions should also be in place. Lifejackets are always a good idea for younger and weaker swimmers using these amenities.

A blob is a large inflatable tube. One person jumps onto it to eject another person already sitting on the blob high into the air and subsequently into the water. In some instances, lifeguards or counselors will blob swimmers or campers. Contact with other people and the bottom is common. To use blobs safely, the following recommendations have been proposed by Markel Insurance Company:

- Blob only one person at a time.
- Enforce a 25-pound (11 kg) maximum weight difference between participants.

- Require at least two lifeguards to manage the blob—one on the tower and one on the water in a watercraft beside the blob.
- Ban all swimming around the blob.
- Ensure 360-degree visibility for lifeguards around the blob. This may necessitate more than two lifeguards.
- Use a safe stairway to climb the tower. Ladders are unsafe.
- Require blobbers to pass a swim test.
- Post clear and concise rules for blob use.
- Lock blob access to prevent unauthorized use when lifeguards are not on duty.

Water trampolines are another popular floating attraction. For safety, a minimum of two lifeguards should be posted on or near the trampoline for surveillance. A swim test should also be required because the trampoline should be placed in 9 feet (2.7 m) of water. As with the blob, collisions with others and the bottom occur frequently, causing fractures and contusions. There should be only one bouncer at a time on the trampoline, and others should be prevented from swimming around the trampoline when in use.

Inflatable icebergs, climbing walls, slides, and obstacle courses should follow the same rules: One person at a time, and 360-degree coverage by lifeguards.

Group Policies

Drowning data reveal that nearly half of all drownings at guarded facilities occur during group outings to pools, water parks, and beaches. Tragically, many of these drownings occur at birthday parties. Adult supervisors of these groups engaging in swimming activities often think they can relax because the lifeguards are watching. Unfortunately, sometimes the lifeguards tend to relax because they believe the adult supervisors are watching. Instead of having double coverage, with both the chaperones and lifeguards watching the group, double trouble results because no one is watching the group. Whenever possible, large groups should register with the beach before the outing. Child-to-adult ratios can then be established, along with water safety guidelines including rules and regulations, hidden hazards, dangerous practices, the buddy system, lifejackets, and so many other vitally important topics. Some state park beaches target large multipassenger vans and busses and board them before allowing the groups onto the beach. With the captive audience seated on the bus, the park ranger provides a powerful water safety orientation for using the beach.

Pets on the Beach

Most beaches need to develop and announce their pet policies so that patrons will not bring their pets with them to the beach. Leaving pets in a car even with the windows slightly open can be fatal because of the extreme and rapid heat buildup in motor vehicles. More rustic and rural beaches tend to allow pets, but some beaches mandate that when owners bring pets to the beach, the pet must be held on a leash no longer than 6 or 8 feet (1.8 or 2.4 m) long. On most managed public beaches in the United States, it appears that banning all pets is the more typical practice for health, safety, and liability reasons. Likewise, many state parks maintain a total ban on pets within the park. When beaches do allow pets such as dogs, they are normally allowed only early in the morning and later in the evening before the swimming beach is open to the public. Dogs and other pets may also be allowed at beaches before the traditional beginning and ending of the summer season (i.e., before Memorial Day weekend and after Labor Day weekend).

Nude (Clothing-Optional) Beaches

Topless swimming and sunbathing are common and not as controversial internationally as they are in the United States. But even in America, clothing-optional beaches are becoming both more popular and accepted. The first public nude beaches in the United States appeared during the 1970s. Statistics reveal nude beaches may even be safer, with fewer fights, fewer sexual assaults, and less other criminal activity than at other beaches. Those participating in nude swimming and sunbathing tend to be older and more into nature and the conservation movement. Although some states and municipalities have laws prohibiting nude beaches, few enforce them. Visual screening when and where possible along with signage noting areas on the beach where nudity may be expected are good ideas. Clothing-optional beaches may also take in additional revenue either through parking fees or entrance admission. For information, contact the American Association for Nude Recreation (1-800-879-6833 or www.aanr.com).

Food and Beverages

Food and drink policies on beaches vary widely throughout the United States and other countries as well. In many regions, bringing food and beverages to the beach is a nonissue and is simply not addressed. In other regions, however, bans on food and drink are strictly enforced. If there are any restrictions on food and beverages, they must be clearly signed. When food and drink are allowed, trash and recycling become issues. Revenue generation can be huge when beaches provide food and beverages to the public. Please refer to chapter 7 for more information on generating revenue with food and beverage services.

Trash Removal and Recycling Programs

Finally, trash removal and recycling programs at beaches and state parks can be so overwhelming that many facilities now simply require that

Dog Beaches

Just as dog parks are sprouting up throughout the United States, so are dog beaches. Because dogs are becoming such an integral part of family life, beaches reserved exclusively for dogs and their owners are becoming more and more popular. Dog beaches typically allow dogs to run on the beach and swim in the water without being on a leash. Of course, owners must be responsible for their dogs' behavior at all times and pick up after them. Dog beaches and dog parks are run similarly, with dog licenses and shots being required. An additional fee may or may not be charged for using the dog beach. Some dog beaches are even fenced off to separate them from adjacent beaches, thus reducing conflicts.

guests take home everything they bring to the beach or park. Trash cans and recycling bins are nonexistent in these locales because the guests are not allowed to leave anything behind when they leave. Plastic garbage bags are often offered free to guests in these parks.

Glass and other breakables should not be allowed at any beaches, pools, and water parks because of the risk of breakage and resulting injuries. It is important that concessionaires serve food and drink items in recyclables, not only to reduce trash and injuries but also to protect the environment. Perhaps every beach and park should follow Florida State Park's lead by proclaiming "every day is Earth Day in the real Florida." Recycling programs significantly help keep beaches clean, reduce trash removal costs, protect the environment, and may also generate funds that can assist in beach maintenance and operations. It is important to use attractive and well-designed containers when encouraging the public to participate in recycling.

Smoking on the Beach

Particularly in the United States, it appears that smoking anywhere in public is becoming more and more difficult. The trend now is to ban all smoking at beaches, not only because of the problem with secondhand smoke but also to reduce the difficult cleanup necessitated by cigarette butts. When smoking is allowed, designated smoking areas with an ample supply of attractive cigarette butt disposals are important. Other countries around the world, with the exception of Canada, do not seem to be as concerned about people smoking in public, including at their beaches, as in the United States.

Alcohol on the Beach

During the summer of 2008, intoxicated beachgoers started so many fights and created so many problems that the City of San Diego, California, banned all alcohol on its beaches. Other beach managers and lifeguards around the country would probably agree that fights, sexual assaults, and drownings at the beach are more often than not fueled by alcohol. Statistics consistently reveal that roughly 50 percent of all drownings are caused by alcohol consumption. Although some beaches and parks ban alcohol, others sell it. It appears that restricting the use of alcohol at beaches and parks can significantly increase the safety and enjoyment of the beach by all.

Driving on the Beach

The popularity of NASCAR today most probably has its roots on the oval track located at Daytona Beach during the early 1900s. Driving on the beach in Florida, North Carolina, Texas, and some other states has long been a tradition in this country. Many beaches today, such as Daytona Beach, still carry on this tradition for a fee. Because of safety and environmental conditions, times, places, and entry points are often specified and sometimes reduced. For more information, contact the Daytona Beach Area Convention and Visitors Bureau at 904-255-0415 or 800-544-0415.

Perhaps not surprisingly, our first roadways in this country were our beaches. Beaches were used for transportation before and during early road construction. Driving on the beach is a tradition on many shorelines dating back to the early days of the automobile. The Outer Banks of North Carolina; the Gulf Coast states; Cape Cod, Massachusetts; and of course, Daytona Beach, Florida, still allow leisurely drives on the beach. The privilege of driving on the beach does come with responsibilities, however. Like any other controversial practice, there are advantages and disadvantages. Some drive on the beach just because it is fun, while others drive on the beach for sport or business purposes. Regardless of the reason, daily and yearly fees are typically assessed to drivers through permits. Although driving on the beach is popular, it also can be damaging and even dangerous. Damage can be reduced by educating and warning drivers as well as channeling and controlling entrance to the beach through limited access points. Driving and nondriving beach zones must be established. Many localities allow beach driving only during the off (winter) months.

In addition to being a potential hazard for humans, vehicles on the beach can also harm animals, plants, and structures. Some of the species most endangered by beach driving include, but are not limited to, the piping plover, least terns, nesting sea turtles, seal pups, sand dunes, and beach vegetation. Figure 9.1 provides safety strategies for driving on the beach.

Fires on the Beach

Basically, the more rural the beach, the more likely that fires will be allowed. On beaches closer to cities and other high-population areas, fires are less likely to be allowed because they can easily become a hazard. In some locales, permits are

Driving on the beach is a tradition and major attraction at some beaches. New Smyrna Beach, Florida, does a wonderful job of managing cars on the beach.

FIGURE 9.1   Safety Strategies for Driving on the Beach

To protect people, animals, vegetation, and property, the following rules and regulations are recommended:

- Lower tire pressure to 20 to 25 psi.
- Maximum speed is 25 mph (40 km/h); 10 to 15 mph (16 to 24 km/h) is preferred.
- Start and stop slowly.
- Stay in tracks made by others.
- Avoid gravel beds and areas prone to high-tide flooding.
- Don't spin your wheels when stuck; reverse first and then go forward.
- Above all, be careful and courteous: Watch out for people, pets, wildlife, dunes, and structures.

Keep the following items in your car when driving on the beach:

- Tire pressure gauge
- Shovel
- Tow strap or strong rope, chain, or cable (14 ft [4.3 m] long; 20,000 lb [9,000 kg] load strength)
- Bumper jack with baseboard
- Flashlight
- First aid kit

required to build a fire on a beach. A popular trend now is to supply strong, raised iron barbecues either in the picnic areas or directly on the beach, closer to the back border. When fires are allowed right on the beach, it is best to supply concrete or metal fire rings to keep the flames contained. Regardless of how heavy the fire rings are, they somehow find their way into the water. When faced with this problem, some beaches offer fire triangles that cannot be rolled into the water. When fires are permitted, safety rules and regulations should be posted, and having buckets of water readily available is important.

Universal Proactive Strategies

Proactive prevention is greatly preferred to reactive rescue and resuscitation. The best lifeguards are the ones who never get wet because of their preemptive actions. This section will help you be a better, more practical risk manager in order to prevent accidents.

Beach Inspections

Daily, weekly, monthly, and seasonal beach inspections are all highly recommended, but perhaps the best assurance of safety is a daily walkabout. Casual daily walkabouts with an eye on safety, the first thing in the morning and the last thing at night, better prepare beach staff to do their jobs.

A quick check of the swimming area, the beach, and the ancillary structures such as restrooms should be conducted before guests arrive at the beach and when the last guests leave in the evening. More comprehensive checklist-type inspections can and should be done on a weekly basis. Of course complete preseason and postseason inspections are recommended, noting changes that need to be accomplished. Regardless of when the inspections are conducted, recommendations and written records of the conditions of the beach, buildings, water, and equipment should all be kept on file.

Water Quality Monitoring

A water quality monitoring program should be put in place to monitor bacteria levels at designated swimming and wading areas. Should bacteria levels exceed recommended limits, swimming should be prohibited, and signs advising the public of the closure should be posted. All swimming beaches should follow their state's health department regulations and guidance advisories with regard to water quality monitoring. Additionally, educational information on preventing recreational water illnesses should be included in safety messages.

Emergency Action Plans

Written emergency action plans (EAPs) are required to be on hand at the beach, and they must be known, understood, and practiced by the entire beach staff. EAP drills should include local emergency response teams whenever possible. The plan should be evaluated once a year and changed as needed in order to meet updated emergency protocols and equipment. The EAP must be beach specific and not simply copied from a water safety agency text or borrowed from another beach, pool, or water park. Some of the essential elements of an acceptable emergency action plan include the following:

- The chain of command and emergency response flowchart, including all primary and secondary responsibilities for all beach staff
- Appropriate placement and use of emergency communication equipment
- Contact numbers of all appropriate law enforcement, fire department, and emergency medical services (EMS) personnel
- Designated first aid station
- Names and contact numbers of all support personnel
- Complete list of all rescue equipment and emergency vehicles to be used
- Search and recovery procedures
- Procedures for crowd control
- Written reports for loss prevention and liability
- Debriefing and accident investigation
- Corrective actions needed in the aftermath of the accident

Accident Reports

When serious injuries occur, particularly those that require additional medical attention, accident forms should be completed, preferably within 24 hours of the accident or illness. These reports should contain only the facts and should not include personal opinions or assess blame. Whenever an injured or ill guest refuses medical attention, it is recommended that the person sign off on the accident reports. Names, addresses, and contact information of the injured party, family members, and witnesses should also be recorded whenever possible. Two copies should be produced for every reported accident or illness; one should be retained by the beach manager, and the other should be forwarded to the appropriate local authorities. Every form should be signed and dated by the person collecting the data and completing the form. Although minor accidents do not normally need to be documented, accident reports should be completed for the following:

- Fatalities
- Resuscitations
- Referrals to hospitals or other medical facilities
- Sickness caused by poor water quality

Shoreline Safety Team

All outdoor employees at beaches should be made part of the shoreline safety team and should begin each summer season with a one-day water safety workshop. This safety team should include the director, operations manager, supervisor, and lead workers; the sheriff's patrol; and the facilities, beach, levee, and maintenance personnel. The key to making this team effective is regularly scheduled and frequent patrols of all access points as well as constant communication among members of the team. Maintenance workers, managers, supervisors, firefighters, and police officers should be mandated to simply walk through the access points daily or on regular patrols. These walk-throughs should be recorded much like the daily log used for checking cleanliness of restrooms.

Beach Closures

Occasionally, severe public health hazards arise at beaches. When this does happen, the beach should be closed to protect the guests. Some safety violations that would be grounds for closing a public beach include but are not limited to the following:

- Rough or dangerous waters including large waves, strong currents, or dangerous marine life
- When required by law, failure to provide adequate supervision (lifeguards)
- When required by law, failure to provide appropriate safety signage and rescue equipment
- When required by law, failure to properly delineate the designated swimming and wading areas
- When required by law, not having sufficient visibility
- Failure to meet water quality standards dictated by the Environmental Protection Agency (EPA) or other local health department
- Having overhead electrical lines near the designated swimming or wading area
- Not supplying potable water or having a contaminated water supply
- Discharging sewage or wastewater directly into or in close proximity to the swimming area
- Any other dangerous or hazardous situation that may be a public health hazard to guests

Rules for Supervising Children

Lost children is probably the number one problem at beaches throughout the world. Finding lost children requires an inordinate amount of time from lifeguards, management, and law enforcement officials. When beach staff are attempting to reunite parents with children, it can detract from the safety of those in the water. Safe and easily recognizable family meeting places make an excellent addition to beaches.

But even more important, parents must be aggressively warned to watch their children when they are in the water, even with lifeguards on duty. Constant, active "reach" supervision needs to be provided by all parents and adult supervisors. Even the best trained and most professional lifeguards cannot watch everyone all the time, and it takes only seconds for a child to drown.

One reason parents need to be reminded to watch their children actively and closely is that in and around their homes, parents get away with supervising passively while multitasking. How

The United States should take the lead from Europe, which sets the standard for family meeting places, found in nearly all public places including beaches. This family meeting place is on the middle of a beach in Italy.

parents supervise their children around their homes is not acceptable at beaches. Parents must be educated that around the water they cannot be distracted and cannot multitask. When adults are supervising children around the water, they should be arm's length away, and visual surveillance of their children should be their only job. It would also be wise to state at what ages children must be accompanied by a responsible adult supervisor. This minimum age requirement varies around the country but tends to gravitate toward 12 years of age before a child can be left unattended at the beach.

In addition to a minimum age for children to be left unattended, adults should be limited to how many young children they can bring to the beach without additional help with supervision. One recommendation is that one adult can supervise only two children at a time. If adults come to the beach with more than two children, they must be accompanied by additional responsible supervisors. And what exactly is a responsible

supervisor? Some suggest that supervisors of children be at least 18 years of age, while others suggest the responsible supervisor simply have a driver's license. Siblings and other relatives tend not to make the best supervisors.

Proactive Strategies at Guarded Beaches

Gone forever are the days when the only requirement to be a lifeguard was a current certification card. Today's lifeguards, particularly beach lifeguards (flat-water or surf), must meet a host of additional requirements and prerequisites before they are hired and while they are employed. When beaches are guarded, perhaps the best resource for lifeguard performance and protocols is the United States Lifesaving Association (www.usla.org). As beach amenities are improved, the possibilities of accidents increase as attendance climbs, and lifeguard numbers and professionalism should likewise increase. Lifeguards should be prescreened on knowledge, swimming, and rescue and resuscitation skills and then retrained during employment through a series of regularly scheduled in-service sessions. Emergency action plans, automated external defibrillators, and oxygen administration are all a part of the professional lifesaving repertoire.

In addition, lifeguards, regardless of age or experience, must be continually supervised, audited, and mentored throughout their employment. Many water safety professionals agree that the safety of the beach is not necessarily in the hands of the lifeguards but in the hands of the lifeguard supervisors. To better supervise lifeguards, lifeguard management courses are now available. The American Red Cross, Ellis and Associates, and StarGuard all offer courses that teach experienced lifeguards how to supervise other lifeguards. It is wise to have at least one experienced certified lifeguard manager who is at least 21 years of age on duty while the beach is open.

Beach Manager

Beach manager is a vitally important position. The beach manager is ultimately responsible for safe operation of the waterfront and, ideally, should be on duty whenever the beach is open to the public. This person not only is in charge of the lifeguards but also must deal with the public and maintain safety as well as decorum on the beach. The beach manager should have experience and training in dealing with the public, in lifeguarding, and in water safety procedures as well as in beach maintenance. A head lifeguard who works directly in concert with the lifeguards on duty may serve as liaison between the beach manager and the lifeguards. It is often preferable to require the head lifeguard to perform actual water surveillance during the day. Whenever possible, it is advisable to have the beach manager seek continuing education in the area of beach management.

Rest Breaks for Patrons and Lifeguards

Perhaps one of the best safety practices at beaches is mandatory rest breaks for swimmers. This practice of course cannot be accomplished at all beaches. Mandatory rest breaks are also more suited for crowded weekends as opposed to weekdays. In-land waterfronts tend to be successful with 10-minute rest breaks on the hour during busy weekends. When the water is cleared, safety messages can be announced, and children can be reunited with their parents for restroom breaks and the reapplication of sunscreen. Most of the lifeguards can also get a brief reprieve from the sun and surveillance at this time, but the water should still be guarded against premature reentry. The rest break is also an excellent time to provide in-service training for the lifeguards by practicing rescue and resuscitation skills in front of the public while they are taking a break from the water. Whenever beach management decides to introduce mandatory patron rest breaks, advance warning is a must. Patrons unaware of the rest break policy quickly become upset when asked to leave the water without prior notification.

Beach Patrols

Patrols by certified lifeguards on motorized vehicles are one of the best safety practices for beaches. Four-wheel-drive ATVs are perhaps the most efficient and least expensive way of providing beach patrols. However, ATVs can carry only one person, cannot carry a victim on a stretcher, and do not have much capacity for rescue and communication equipment. Surf beaches tend to use four-wheel-drive trucks because rescues and emergencies are much more common. Beach patrols are especially recommended for beaches where lifeguards are not on duty in elevated stations.

It must be remembered that along with beach vehicles come maintenance and storage issues. Both additional requirements can be costly in terms of structures and space. If beach vehicles are a must but funds are short, it may be wise to solicit donors who could then provide appropriate vehicles in return for advertising on the vehicles themselves. Likewise, free storage nearby may also be found in return for advertising or other services.

Proactive Strategies at Unguarded Beaches

Whenever possible, when lifeguards will not be on duty, safety patrols are highly recommended. Lifeguards in four-wheel-drive vehicles or ATVs driving up and down a beach can provide an authoritative presence to help ensure people are using the beach wisely and to provide rescue and resuscitation efforts when necessary. Older, more experienced professionals on beach patrol may in some instances be more effective than younger, less experienced lifeguards on duty who are not adequately trained, mentored, and supervised. Especially if the beach patrol has law enforcement capabilities, they are more likely to have a positive effect on beach safety. The town of South Haven, Michigan, is one lakefront community that has successfully removed its lifeguards and replaced them with beach safety patrols. In addition to motorized patrols on the beach, parking attendants located high above the beach assist with water safety concerns by radioing beach patrols and police as needed. Likewise, Pennsylvania has moved from guarded beaches to unguarded beaches at all its state park lakes. Pennsylvania instituted an open swim program that requires swimmers to stay within the designated buoyed safe swimming area and follow the open-swimming rules.

Although lifeguards are not recommended for approved wading areas at this time, regular and consistent shoreline safety patrols are highly recommended. The Army Corps of Engineers has safely maintained perhaps more swimming beaches in the United States than any other single agency. It has accomplished a tremendous safety record *without* lifeguards but with good education, signage, and frequent patrols.

Summary

Operational considerations for both safety and enjoyment vary from beach to beach and from locale to locale. Similar beach practices may be accepted in some parts of the country but completely banned in others. For the operations and activities most suitable in certain beach communities, perhaps it is best to visit beaches in other communities of similar size and demographics to see what works and what does not. Determine rules about beach attire, noise, games, balls, throwing, running, selling and consuming products, and a multitude of other issues before the public uses the beach. Other concerns include riding horses, building fires, setting off fireworks, and using metal detectors. Contact other beaches to find where they stand on these issues.

Water Quality and Beach Maintenance

10

Beachgoers are no longer satisfied with water that is simply clear; they are now more concerned with water that is clean. Clean sand and water form a recipe for success when it comes to the beach experience. But clear, clean water is not easy to accomplish in many cases. Pristine beaches are a worthy goal to aspire to, and this chapter shows the way.

Adequately informing guests when the water is unhealthy is important. In 1996, more than 2,500 beaches in the United States posted water quality warnings or closed completely for at least a day because the waters were contaminated (Griffiths 1999). Unlike swimming pools and water parks, beach water, whether it is fresh or marine water, is not usually filtered or disinfected. Too often, beachgoers expect open water to be just as clean as chemically treated swimming pool water. More recently, the public has become aware of polluted water at beaches through beach closings publicized in the media. No doubt, the Internet has also highlighted news of polluted water and closed beaches. Water quality is now becoming an important factor in deciding which beach is selected by beachgoers. Water that is clean, clear, and safe is now of vital importance, more so than ever before, perhaps because of our renewed interest in a clean and green society.

Many countries around the world simply do not clean or maintain their beaches. A colleague in New Zealand, when asked why they don't clean their beaches, quickly exclaimed, "Why should we? It's a beach!" The flora and fauna and other particulate matter that wash up on the sands are considered by many to be the natural life cycle of the beach and the water. But for those who spend great sums of money to be on white sandy beaches, beach cleaning and maintenance are preferred. White, pristine, groomed beaches come at a great cost, however. Maintaining pretty beaches not only requires a great deal of time, energy, money, and specialized equipment but also can cause ecological damage. Nesting birds, turtles, and other animals can all be adversely affected by beach cleaning.

This chapter first focuses on recreational water illnesses (RWIs) that may be contracted at beaches and how to prevent them. Later in the chapter, nuisance plant, animal, and human influences are discussed from a safety and enjoyment perspective. Finally, we present information about cleaning, sanitizing, and grooming beaches.

Recreational Water Illnesses (RWIs)

According to the Centers for Disease Control and Prevention (CDC), recreational water illnesses (RWIs) are spread by swallowing, breathing, or otherwise having contact with contaminated water from swimming pools, spas, lakes, rivers, or oceans. For the purposes of this book, the discussion of RWIs will be restricted to open water, whether it is fresh or salt (marine) water. RWIs can cause a wide variety of symptoms including but not limited to gastrointestinal, skin, ear, respiratory, eye, and neurological issues as well as wound infections. The most common RWI by far is diarrhea. Young children, pregnant women, and people with compromised immune systems (people with HIV or AIDS, organ recipients, chemotherapy patients) are most susceptible to RWIs. Serious illnesses can result in these groups when RWIs are contracted. Cryptosporidium, a common and troublesome RWI, can be life threatening in persons with weakened immune systems. In addition, it appears that marine (salt) waters are more likely to produce RWIs than are freshwater rivers, lakes, and ponds.

Lakes, rivers, and oceans can become contaminated with infectious bacteria from sewage, animal waste, water runoff after heavy rainfalls, fecal accidents, and germs rinsed off infected swimmers while swimming. To avoid RWIs, patrons should never swallow water when at the beach. Swimming after heavy rainfalls is not advised, nor is swimming during droughts in small impoundments of water with poor circulation. When in doubt, contact the local health department regulating the beach in question. Health departments test the water for harmful bacteria regularly and post the results. The good news is that, in general, open waters are much cleaner today than they were 50 years ago because of the Clean Water Act, the BEACH Act, and other forms of clean water legislation. Second, polluted waters often make swimmers sick, but fatalities rarely occur, unless of course the swimmers or waders affected were high risk.

Unfortunately, many Americans swim with diarrhea, one of the leading causes of water contamination. Swimmers with diarrhea can infect other swimmers if they swallow water. Conversely, all people have roughly .14 gram of feces on their bottoms, which can contaminate recreational waters, particularly during busy, hazy, hot, and humid days. If water is not swallowed, sickness does not usually follow.

Six PLEAs to Prevent Water Contamination

The CDC has developed six steps for both swimmers and parents to prevent both water contamination and RWIs.

Three PLEAs for all swimmers:

Please don't swim when you have diarrhea. You can spread germs in the water and make other people sick. This is especially important for children in the water.

Please don't swallow the water. In fact, avoid getting water in your mouth.

Please practice good hygiene. Take a shower before swimming, and wash your hands after using the toilet and changing diapers. Germs on your body end up in the water.

Three PLEAs for parents with young children:

Please take your kids to the bathroom often, and check and clean diapers often.

Please change diapers in a bathroom or diaper-changing area and not near the water.

Germs can end up in the water and contaminate others.

Please wash your child thoroughly, especially the rear end, with soap and water before swimming. Everyone has invisible amounts of fecal matter on their bottoms that ends up in the water.

Adapted from the CDC.

Pathogens

More specifically, health concerns at beaches exist because of pathogens. A pathogen is simply a disease-producing microorganism. Microorganisms exist in all terrestrial and aquatic ecosystems. The small subset of microorganisms that cause human disease is called human pathogens. The source of human pathogens is usually the feces of humans and other warm-blooded animals.

Enteric pathogens are those that follow the fecal–oral route (i.e., they are first found in feces and then swallowed). Naturally, not swallowing infected waters is of paramount importance. Recreational waters contain three groups of gastrointestinal pathogens that can adversely affect humans: bacteria, viruses, and protozoans. A primary bacterial source at beaches is feces from people and other warm-blooded animals, including agricultural fecal waste and domestic waste discharge. Bacteria in feces that are waterborne include the coliform group, streptococcus, lactobacillus, staphylococcus, and clostridium. Fortunately, most bacteria are not pathogenic or disease causing.

Viruses are a group of infectious agents that require a host in which to live and reproduce.

The most significant virus group affecting water quality and human health grows and reproduces in the gastrointestinal tract of people and infected animals. These enteric viruses are excreted in feces and include hepatitis A, rotaviruses, caliciviruses (noroviruses), adenoviruses, enteroviruses, and reoviruses. Pathogenic protozoans constitute approximately one-third of the 35,000 protozoans and are found in the feces of warm-blooded animals and humans. Two protozoan species of major concern because of their waterborne properties are Giardia lamblia and Cryptosporidium parvum.

Bacterial Indicators

Bacterial indicators are used to measure fecal contamination in recreational waters. Bacterial indicator organisms provide evidence of the presence or absence of fecal waste and the potential presence of pathogenic organisms that survive under similar conditions. The Environmental Protection Agency (EPA) now suggests using enterococcus or E. coli for freshwater beaches while recommending only enterococcus for marine (salt) waters. Weekly testing and testing immediately after heavy rainfalls are highly recommended. Using total and fecal coliform levels is no longer considered appropriate in these waters.

In regard to water testing, the EPA

- recommends weekly monitoring of bacteria levels at most beaches,
- suggests preemptive closing at certain areas following storm events, and
- requires prompt public notification of elevated bacteria levels.

Waters that contain significant fecal contamination can infect swimmers and waders by way of enteric pathogens taking the fecal–oral routes. These include the following:

- Bacteria that can cause cholera, salmonellosis, shigellosis, and gastroenteritis
- Viruses that can cause disease-like infectious hepatitis, gastroenteritis, and intestinal diseases
- Protozoans that can cause diseases such as amoebic dysentery, cryptosporidiosis, and giardiasis

RWI Prevention Strategies

The CDC recommends five vitally important areas to improve in order to reduce the risk of contamination and RWIs:

1. Clean hygiene facilities
2. Bathroom break policies
3. Group use policies for large youth groups
4. Posting and distributing healthy swimming information
5. RWI outbreak response plan

Clean Hygiene Facilities

Lasting impressions of any public or private facility are often made in the restrooms. Clean, attractive, and well-stocked facilities leave patrons with a strong positive impression, while dirty, untidy facilities have a significant negative affect. Are your bathrooms and changing rooms adequate in number? Are the facilities close to both the parking lot and the water? Are the facilities clean and well maintained? Would you walk barefoot in them just like your patrons? These are the types of questions good beach managers ask themselves while managing their beaches.

Bathroom Break Policies

Let's be perfectly honest here: Way too many adults and children "go" in the water. Good beach management emphasizes preventive education by letting both parents and children know that the restrooms are provided to reduce illness. Parents should take their children to the restrooms often to go to the bathroom as well as to wash their hands with soap and water. Where possible, hourly bathroom breaks are highly recommended at smaller flat-water lakes and ponds. These 10- to 15-minute breaks are a good time to introduce water safety concepts and possibly present a rescue scenario. At the very least, safety and bathroom breaks should be attempted on weekends.

Group Use Policies for Large Youth Groups

If large groups of toddlers and younger children will be using your beach, particularly if some of these children are in diapers or not potty trained, strongly consider providing a healthy swimming orientation, both verbally and in writing, before the children access the beach.

Day care centers must be particularly vigilant in this area. Once again, the CDC is perhaps the best resource on this vitally important topic: See www.cdc.gov.healthyswimming.org. Group use policies are very important not only for hygiene but also for water safety. Be certain to stress rules and regulations as well as the water safety responsibilities of the teachers, counselors, and parents attending these group trips.

Posting and Distributing Healthy Swimming Information

In addition to talking to user groups about preventing RWIs through good practices and providing written handouts when possible, posting these vitally important suggestions for everyone to see is highly recommended.

RWI Outbreak Response Plan

Although most beaches have emergency action plans (EAPs) in place for water emergencies at the beach, many unfortunately do not have an RWI outbreak response plan. Although prevention is always the best policy, if an RWI outbreak occurs at your beach, are you prepared? The first step in developing an RWI response plan is to contact your local health department that tests the beach water. They will offer assistance in finding the best way to post information and close swimming facilities. Selecting a spokesperson who is well versed in the area of RWIs and who can speak accurately and effectively to both the public and the media is also of vital importance. The spokesperson must be trained to deliver a clear and consistent message about beach closures, and this person should be selected and trained before the possibility of any beach closure.

Particularly if a beach is in a pollution-prone area, appropriate closure signage should be made up and ready for posting before an incident. Many beaches use beach flags for a variety of conditions. One way of alerting the public of beach closings before they get out of their cars is to fly a flag specifically for polluted water. Beach closures should also be posted on the appropriate websites and sent out on pertinent e-mail lists. Press releases also need to be sent to TV, radio, and the print media when it can be done in a timely fashion. If RWI or pollution outbreaks are common, perhaps a telephone hotline should be developed just for water quality and healthy swimming information. It would also be helpful to speak to other beach managers who have had outbreaks in the past so you can better prepare for the possibility in the future. Finally, it is extremely important to develop a good relationship with your health officials before an outbreak. If an outbreak does occur, assist with the investigation willingly.

Urban and Agricultural Sources of Pollution

Much of what has been written so far in this chapter deals with human sources of pollution. It is important to know that urban runoff and agricultural and wildlife sources of pollution can also adversely affect beachgoers. Urban runoff is caused by the flushing of decaying organic matter left in streets, gutters, and storm drains after sustained, heavy rainfall. Concerning agricultural sources of pollution, dairy cows can discharge up to 55 pounds (25 kg) of manure per day. If cows are allowed to pollute streams in the watershed upstream of the swimming beach, significant pollution can be produced.

Likewise, whenever manure is applied as fertilizer to farm fields in the winter and spring in the watershed, nearby beaches will eventually receive large coliform counts produced from the manure. Fertilizers can also have an adverse effect on the watershed. Nitrogen-based fertilizers typically promote algae growth and deplete oxygen stores, which leads to unhealthy waters. Actually, any sediment from farm fields that goes into beach waters can increase the likelihood of reducing both water clarity and water quality.

When it comes to wildlife, the Canada goose remains the largest source of pollution. Our resident Canada goose population contaminates our beaches, lakes, rivers, and oceans. Each Canada goose excretes between 1 and 2 pounds (.5 to 1 kg) per day. Considering the size of goose flocks, that's a lot of poop! There are other sources of wildlife pollution, but Canada geese are the most significant across the country. Particularly for in-land flat-water beaches, beaver dam impoundments can hold significant amounts of contamination, and when these ponds are broken up, as they often are, the pollution can find its way to the beach.

Other Waterborne Concerns

Some water quality issues do not produce major recreational water illnesses but rather damage the ecosystem in the water and reduce the aesthetics and enjoyment of the beach.

Algae Blooms

Algae blooms can be particularly troublesome for swimmers in open water. Blue-green algae are typically found in freshwater lakes and ponds, while red algae are usually found in the oceans. Although hundreds of different algae exist and are an important base of the marine chain, only a few species produce toxins that are harmful to humans and pets.

Blue-Green Algae

Blue-green algae blooms (Anabaena, Microcystis) are often found in freshwater lakes and ponds but can occur in some marine waters during drought conditions. Blue-green algae tend to proliferate when high nutrient levels are introduced to the water from agricultural runoff and other sources. Particularly when water is stagnant and temperatures rise, conditions are ideal for massive algae blooms. When water containing high levels of blue-green algae is swallowed, flulike symptoms can occur within hours. In some geographical regions, permits may be obtained to use copper sulfate in waters where blue-green algae tend to bloom heavily.

Red Algae

Red algae, or red tides, now threaten most coastal states. Red algae tides are actually blooms and tend to occur during warm weather in relatively calm coastal waters. Red tides are most probably produced by excessive nutrients running off into coastal waters. The neurotoxins found in red tides kill fish, birds, and invertebrates. Humans consuming large amounts of shellfish can be inadvertently affected by these red tides, sometimes with fatal results.

Swimmer's Itch (Schistosome Dermatitis)

Swimmer's itch is caused by a freshwater parasite and can produce intense itching and rash. It is common in midwestern lakes but is now spreading throughout the United States. The parasites that cause swimmer's itch are found in duck droppings, and people visiting the beach become the accidental hosts. With the migration of infected ducks, the disease is spreading and difficult to control.

Seabather's Eruption

Often referred to as sea lice, seabather's eruption is an itchy dermatitis usually restricted to the swimsuit areas of the body. It is caused when the larvae of the thimble jellyfish become trapped under the bathing suit or other garments worn in the water. Frequent washing of suits and clothing worn in the water, sunscreen, and suntan lotion may all help reduce seabather's eruption. Antihistamine and cortisone creams should help relieve the itch.

Creeping Eruption

This condition is easily contracted on coastal beaches and other sandy areas. The cause of creeping eruption is quite simple to explain: Free-roaming dogs and cats often defecate in these sandy areas. Their feces may contain parasitic worms, which are picked up by humans on bare feet and other body parts exposed when beachgoers step, sit, and lie on the sand. Children playing in the sand are particularly prone to creeping eruption. Skin rash at the point of contact is the main symptom. Medication prescribed by a physician is needed to cure the rash. To prevent creeping eruption, dogs and cats should be kept off the beach, and it is recommended that beachgoers use blankets and footwear. Covering sand in play areas at night might also help.

Controlling Aquatic Plants and Animal Pests at Beaches

Not all water quality problems at beaches arise directly from pollution. Numerous plants and animals cause problems at beaches and may encroach on the quality of the beach experience.

Geese and Waterfowl Control

Humans are not the only ones who enjoy a day at the beach. Unfortunately, many birds and waterfowl are also attracted to beaches for a variety of reasons and can create concerns for humans. Many parks and golf courses throughout

Web Resources for Water Quality

Environmental Protection Agency: www.epa.gov/ost/beaches

Natural Resources Defense Council: www.nrdc.org/water/oceans

U.S. Centers for Disease Control and Prevention: www.cdc.gov.healthyswimming.org

Aquatics International magazine: www.aquaticsintl.com

Aquatic Safety Research Group: www.aquaticsafetygroup.com

Zero Waste Alliance: www.Zerowaste.org

the country have a huge problem with Canada geese, and many beaches experience the same problems. Short grass, water, sand, leftover picnic food, hunting restrictions (Migratory Bird Treaty Act), and favorable agricultural practices all provide safe havens for Canada geese. Because conditions are so friendly and favorable, many geese no longer migrate but rather have taken up permanent residence throughout the United States; as a result, the Canada geese population continues to grow in this country. Canada Geese can be a nuisance to many people, and they may pose a health hazard to swimmers because large flocks produce large amounts of fecal coliform, which often end up in swimming areas after heavy rains. More specifically, goose feces may be linked to salmonella, chlamydia, and swimmer's itch, but the health risks are still being debated.

Many different nonlethal methods can be used to keep Canada geese off beaches, off lawns, and out of parks. Over the long haul, however, no one tactic may be foolproof. Using border collies, who tend to be tireless and love exercising, is perhaps more effective than the other measures mentioned here. Another fairly effective and humane corrective measure is birth control through egg addling (oiling). This is a sophisticated method using volunteers to oil the eggs so they will not hatch. In addition to border collies and egg addling, chemical aversion agents, fencing and landscaping barriers, pyrotechnics, balloons, high-frequency sounds, electric fences, artificial cygnets, owls, foxes, noisemakers, and other methods have all been used with limited success. Finally, killing the geese outright may be the most effective technique, but it is controversial. Although the federal Fish and Wildlife Service has granted permission to hunt the geese in some regions, there are many opponents who protest this action vehemently. At the very least, a strong ban on feeding Canada geese should be in place at every park and beach.

Chemical Treatment of Lakes and Ponds

As temperatures rise and attendance increases, in many cases, so do fecal coliform counts. In these cases, sometimes the only way to keep the lake open to the public is by treating with chlorine to lower bacteria counts to an acceptable level. With appropriate approval and proper permits, often a grid piping system installed just below the sand can be used to deliver chlorine only within the designated swimming areas in lakes with bacteria.

Likewise when algae, weeds, or other plant nuisances begin to proliferate, copper sulfate (bluestone) can be used to effectively kill the plant life. Permission and permits are usually required before applying this inexpensive yet effective chemical. Swimming should be suspended during and shortly after the application of copper sulfate.

Aeration has been known to reduce algae, weeds, odors, sediments, and bacteria levels and to improve water quality in general. Particularly for smaller swimming ponds and lakes that also may become stagnant, aeration may make sense.

Water fountains can be added as part of the aeration system, which should also be a bonus aesthetically. They can be an attractive nuisance, however, particularly when placed in deeper water, greater than 5 feet (1.5 m). When fountains are used at a swimming beach, swimmers should not be allowed to access them because the falling water and surface agitation may hide swimmers under the fountains. They may also attract younger and more novice swimmers. Any swimmers getting into trouble under water fountains are not only difficult to detect but also difficult to recover and rescue, making resuscitation efforts less likely to succeed.

Beach Maintenance

Early morning hours are typically the best time of day to clean beaches. Usually, a beach maintenance crew cleans all beaches, bike trails, sidewalks, boardwalks, and similar structures and also takes care of trash removal. Written policies and practices should be developed and followed by the beach maintenance crew. Naturally, more personnel are needed during the peak season than in the off-season.

Waterline Raking and Cleaning

Perhaps the most important area to clean on the beach is the waterline, where the beach sand meets the water's edge. Cleaning the waterline is important because that is where most of the waterborne debris collects, and that is where most people congregate just before and just after getting in and out of the water. Depending on the length of the beach and the size and amount of material deposited at the waterline, cleaning can be accomplished by a variety of tools, from simple hand rakes to large, sophisticated machinery. Many beach crews clean the waterline first thing in the morning, as often as seven days a week, depending of course on the amount of flotsam produced overnight.

The waterline does not require as much attention off-season or when attendance is low. Overaggressive beach raking can have an adverse effect on bird and animal feeding and mating practices. Particularly when endangered species use the beach, beach raking may be prohibited altogether.

Beach Sanitizing

Beach sanitizing refers to mechanically screening or filtering the finest of particulates from beach sand. Automated beach sanitizers remove small shards of glass, plastic, and other fine particles. Beach sanitizing is particularly important in playground areas, sand volleyball courts, sand soccer fields, and other beach activity areas. Proper beach sanitizing leaves a very soft and safe sand underfoot and is much appreciated by those playing vigorously in the sand.

Adopt-a-Beach Programs

Regardless of the type of beach or its location, daily litter, whether washed up on the shoreline from afar or dropped by beachgoers, seems to be a consistent and persistent problem. Food, paper products, plastics, cans, bottles, straws, and ciga-

Waterline raking is often accomplished by hand with hand rakes. Although it is effective, the work is difficult and takes a great deal of time. Automated mechanical raking devices are much faster and easier to use, although much more expensive.

rette butts can not only quickly clutter a beach but also be safety hazards to both humans and animals alike. Flotsam, which is debris floating in the water, can pose threats to swimmers and waders. Retrieval of flotsam should be left to lifeguards or qualified beach staff. At surf beaches, flotsam can quickly become projectiles that can seriously injure guests, and in some instances, the presence of flotsam can close beaches. To combat litter on the beach, Adopt-a-Beach programs have worked well. School groups, senior citizens, businesses, and nonprofit agencies are all appropriate groups for keeping beaches clean, reducing workloads of beach staff, reducing costs, and reporting beach abuse. Well-organized Adopt-a-Beach programs can also identify the source of beach litter, therefore eliminating it in the future.

Beach Cleanups

The first coastal cleanups in the United States began on Texas beaches in 1986. At that time, nearly 3,000 volunteers collected nearly 124 tons (112,000 kg) of trash. In 2007, more than 378,000 volunteers from around the world participated in the International Coastal Cleanup and collected 6 million pounds (2.7 million kg) of debris from more than 33,000 miles (53,000 km) of shoreline. That translates to approximately 182 pounds (83 kg) of trash per mile (1.6 km). Americans accounted for more than half of all volunteers (190,000 volunteers from 45 states). California residents led the way with 22 percent of the U.S. volunteers.

The Ocean Conservancy cites five major areas of trash production in coastal waters (www.oceanconservancy.org):

1. Shoreline and recreational activities. Somewhat surprisingly, most marine debris comes from land-based recreation. Food consumption, beachgoers, picnics, sports and recreation, and festivals all significantly contribute to ocean debris. Generic litter from streets, parking lots, and storm drains also finds its way to the open water after heavy rains.

2. Ocean and waterway activities. All types of boating and fishing contribute to ocean debris. Sources of pollution include recreational fishing and boating; commercial fishing; cargo, military, and cruise ship operations; and offshore industries such as oil drilling.

3. Smoking-related activities. Smoking pollutes not only the air but our waters as well. Improper disposal of cigarette filters, cigar tips, and tobacco packaging all contribute significantly on both land and sea.

4. Dumping activities. Both legal and illegal dumping of building materials and household appliances leads to ocean debris.

5. Medical and personal hygiene. When people dispose of medical and personal hygiene products in toilets and city streets, these items often enter the waste stream through sewer systems and have an adverse effect on water quality.

International beach cleanups have three major goals:

1. Clean the beaches by removing debris from in and around open-water areas.

2. Collect information about specific forms of debris, including their sources.

3. Educate people about water and beach debris to reduce the problem and make our beaches and waters safer, cleaner, and more enjoyable.

Beach cleanups would certainly become less laborious and perhaps even unnecessary if people created less waste by reusing and recycling. A zero-waste policy in America would certainly be beneficial for cleaner and healthier land and water in our country. We can all make a difference in this regard. By participating in recycling efforts and beach cleanups, our beaches will become cleaner, safer, and more enjoyable.

Beach Sand Grooming

Beach sand grooming refers to the cleaning of the entire beach and usually requires heavy machinery. The type and amount of machinery vary with the size and popularity of the beach. In many instances, the entire beach does not need to be groomed daily and may require grooming only once a week. When beach sand grooming is a priority, large agricultural tractors are often used in combination with hydraulic rakes and screens to clean the entire beach. Good sand screens can sift and clean sand as deep as 6 inches (15 cm) and typically remove particles of half an inch (1.3 cm) or larger.

Girl Scouts clean up the beach for the Ohio Department of Natural Resources. Volunteer programs such as these save on maintenance costs and provide a valuable educational experience.

Beach Rebuilding

Erosion produced after large storms and during the off-season often creates the need for massive rebuilding of beaches. Beach rebuilding requires large equipment such as dump trucks and bulldozers. Sand is often brought in from other areas on the beach or even other beaches where excess sand has accumulated. The sand is dumped into large canyons and holes on the beach produced by storms and then groomed and sanitized once it is leveled. When sand dunes have been damaged by storms, they too need to be rebuilt.

Organic materials such as kelp can sometimes be used as the base for newly constructed sand dunes. The sand dunes on the Outer Banks of North Carolina were entirely bulldozed up from the beaches many years ago to protect properties from high water.

Storm Cleanup

In addition to eroding beaches, inclement weather typically deposits debris. Particularly where rivers and creeks meet lakes and oceans, a tremendous amount of debris can be deposited and requires days to remove. After large storms,

daily beach cleaning is suspended until all storm debris is cleared from beaches, lagoons, bays, and marinas.

Beach Cleaning Equipment

Most Americans enjoy pristine, white, clean, well-contoured, and manicured beach sand free of debris. To accomplish this, many highly technological beach cleaning apparatus are available. Beach cleaning is now an art and a science; it takes both time and money to produce comfortable, clean, and aesthetically pleasing beaches. The cost to produce pleasing beaches is more than just financial, however. Regular beach cleaning with heavy machinery can endanger the piping plover, least terns, nesting sea turtles, seal pups, beach vegetation, and other beach flora and fauna. To protect beach animals and vegetation, beach cleaning should be performed carefully and selectively. Cleaning more populated beaches may be preferable to cleaning all beaches. In other words, mechanically clean urban or cosmopolitan beaches, but do not mechanically clean natural and transitional beaches. Interestingly, many countries around the world do not clean their beaches at all, believing that beaches in their natural state are a vitally important part of the ecosystem.

Depending on the size of the beach, many varied forms of beach cleaning equipment can be used, from hand rakes to clean the waterline to heavy machinery. Some of the equipment is listed here:

- Hand tools including leaf rakes, hard rakes, leaf blowers, and shovels
- Bulldozers
- Pickup trucks
- Dump trucks
- Parking lot sweepers
- Broom, street, and sidewalk sweepers
- Tow or pull behinds
- Loaders
- Surf rakes
- Disks
- Beach Kings
- Articulated loaders

Protecting Marine Wildlife

Much of what has been written so far has addressed making beaches and waters safer and more pleasurable for humans. But what can be a nuisance to humans can actually kill marine life, particularly marine mammals and birds. For instance, plastic beverage rings are particularly notorious for killing both marine birds and mammals by strangulation. Adopt-a-Beach programs can be especially helpful seasonally and between international beach cleanups. Although this text strongly encourages regular beach cleaning, volunteers, paid staff, and beachgoers in general must exercise caution if they detect injured or entangled birds, fish, or mammals at the beach.

The California Marine Mammal Center has developed six steps when injured, entangled, or stranded marine life are encountered. They recommend the following:

1. Do not attempt to get close to stranded, entangled, or injured animals. Keep your distance. Keep others away, and call the appropriate authorities.

2. Do not attempt to assist young animals such as seal pups that appear to be abandoned. Many mothers leave their young temporarily to find food for their babies.

3. Large mammals such as dolphins and whales require assistance from professionals. Call the appropriate authorities, and stand by to help with water and shade for these animals, but keep your distance until instructed by professional responders.

4. Record as much information as possible (size, shape, color, wounds, tags) before contacting authorities. Accurate information will assist rescue workers.

5. Know the exact location of the animal. Name the beach and mention landmarks in order to expedite the emergency response.

6. The first five steps also apply to disabled animals in the water.

Summary

A clean beach is a pretty beach, and most beachgoers prefer beaches that are clean and litter free. But there is a delicate balance between finely manicuring the beach and causing harm to the environment. Visiting other beaches in your locale to ask about their beach maintenance program is highly recommended.

Safety Practices at Guarded Beaches

With contributions by Robert E. Ogoreuc

The new and interesting lifeguarding and lifesaving information provided here is an attempt to connect the dots and fill in the gaps that exist between other authoritative water safety texts. The goal of this chapter is to make beaches safer through better trained lifeguards and more educated guests.

Whether beaches are unguarded or guarded, a wealth of safety practices and procedures should be considered to increase safety for swimming and wading. The American Red Cross, YMCA of the USA, Ellis and Associates, StarGuard, and the National Aquatic Safety Company (NASCO) all provide excellent information for lifeguards. However, for water safety information specifically regarding beaches, the United States Lifesaving Association is perhaps the best resource. Utilizing as many water safety texts as possible to develop best practices is an excellent idea. This chapter does not discuss specific rescue techniques but rather offers general suggestions for surveillance and vigilance, many of which are not found in other water safety texts. Not all beaches have lifeguards, and for those that do not, a special set of water safety procedures should be considered. Finally, lifeguards do not guarantee patron safety and are not a replacement for parental supervision. Whether or not lifeguards are on duty, nonswimmers must exercise caution in the water, and parents must actively and aggressively watch their children, in, on, and around the water.

Lifeguard Requirements and Competency

Lifeguards today are required to have so much more than just their certification cards stating their competencies in lifeguarding, first aid, CPR, and oxygen management. When the decision is made by beach management to supply lifeguards at a waterfront, a long list of additional requirements beyond basic certifications comes into play as dictated by the standard of care. Background checks, vision tests, prejob knowledge, water skill tests, rescue and resuscitation equipment training, prejob orientations, continual in-service training, and unannounced audits all are highly recommended and may even be required for many beach lifeguards.

Although most surf lifeguards are well trained and well paid, flat-water beach guards typically do not receive the salaries or training they deserve. This may be because nonsurf guards are considered seasonal help and are not unionized. So although much is required of lifeguards, for the most part, they are overworked and underpaid. In addition, many people, particularly at smaller flat-water beaches and waterfronts,

consider lifeguards to be babysitters rather than highly trained emergency care professionals and only want to pay them and train them accordingly. However, when an aquatic emergency does occur, those paying lifeguard wages expect a rapid and professional response, even though their initial perception was a part-time babysitter. Mature, experienced, full-time lifeguard professionals tend to be found at surf beaches, particularly those with year-round swimming weather. Nonsurf, seasonal beach lifeguards tend to be younger, part-time employees who require constant supervision and mentoring while on duty.

Perhaps the best defense against drowning and other catastrophic injuries is swimming near a lifeguard. Unfortunately, drowning and other accidents do occur at guarded beaches, and many occur outside the designated swimming areas. A much higher percentage of incidents seem to occur after the lifeguards leave the beach for the day and are off duty, leaving the beach unprotected. What the lifeguard does while she is providing visual surveillance is of paramount importance when protecting guests and is the major emphasis of this chapter. Proactive prevention through visual surveillance rather than reactive rescue and resuscitation should be the goal of every lifeguard and will be highlighted in the following pages.

Awareness of Drowning Causes

Drowning prevention should be easy to accomplish, but in reality, it is not. The drowning process is quiet and quick, and many drowning scenarios are unique. Some people will spend some time struggling on the surface, while others will quickly and quietly sink. Some people jump, dive, or plunge below the surface without ever resurfacing, hence the term *plunge downers*. Regardless of the actual drowning process, after two minutes of submersion, effective resuscitation is difficult at best. In the open-water environment, this is particularly troublesome because a lack of water clarity can quickly doom the victim.

Although every drowning scenario is different, some similarities do exist: Males drown significantly more often than females; Native Americans, African Americans, and Hispanics drown at a much higher rate than whites. Depending on their age, drowning is either the leading or the second-leading cause of death in children. Those with seizure disorders are nearly 20 times more likely to drown than those who don't have seizure disorders. That is why it is so important for a person with epilepsy to swim with a partner, wear a type III lifejacket, and inform the lifeguard that he has a seizure disorder. Medical abnormalities such as long QT syndrome, the RyR2 gene, and hypertrophic cardiomyopathy all kill people in the water. Unfortunately, coroners and medical examiners state their findings are "consistent with drowning."

Although it is easy to blame parents for not actively supervising their child when they tragically lose a child to drowning, it must be remembered that passive supervision or supervising while multitasking is common in our society. This behavior is difficult to change.

Drowning rates can be drastically reduced when all children learn to swim at an early age (4 to 6 years) and when those under the age of 12 or under 48 inches (122 cm) tall who cannot swim wear properly fitting type III PFDs.

The United States Lifesaving Association (USLA) describes the drowning process in an open-water environment as follows:

1. Distress
2. Panic
3. Submersion

USLA does note, however, that the first two stages are often absent, and the victim can quickly and suddenly submerge without warning. Because the process is so short, it is vitally important for open-water lifeguards to detect distress and panic before the victim submerges.

The distress stage is relatively short, and depending on a swimmer's ability, the distress reaction may vary. Some distressed victims may wave for help or float on their backs. They may last on the surface for seconds or a few minutes. Distress is common during rip current encounters. Rip currents account for approximately 80 percent of all rescues at surf beaches.

Panic is an overwhelming and unreasonable fear that overcomes near-drowning victims. This may or may not follow the distress phase. Once a swimmer or nonswimmer enters the panic stage, she is nearly incapacitated with fear and almost entirely dependent on others to save her. If not rescued in a speedy fashion, she will submerge quickly because a panicked person rapidly loses buoyancy. Once a near-drowning victim submerges, only a two-minute window of opportunity for successful recovery and resuscitation exists.

Sudden Submersion Syndrome

Good swimmers don't often drown; rather, they die of other major medical maladies. Some of these medical maladies do not show up at autopsy, and coroners and medical examiners routinely rule "drowning." Sudden cardiac arrest, seizure, stroke, trauma, drugs, alcohol, and others can all quickly kill a swimmer on or near the surface. When this happens, the victim suddenly submerges, and the lungs subsequently fill with water. Sudden submersion syndrome is difficult to detect and impossible to prevent. But because coroners rule "drowning" in these cases, lifeguards need to be alert and responsive in a professional and timely fashion so they are not blamed for the supposed drowning.

Shallow-Water Blackout

Shallow-water blackout (SWB) can often be a cause of sudden submersion syndrome. These blackout scenarios can cause either unconsciousness, which can lead to drowning, or sudden death. SWB requires competitive, repetitive breath holding or underwater swimming that involves hyperventilation (overbreathing). Although SWB typically occurs in standard competitive swimming pools, it does occur in the open water. To prevent shallow-water blackout and sudden submersion syndrome, prolonged, competitive, and repetitive breath holding and underwater swimming should be banned at all aquatic facilities.

Surveillance and Vigilance

The primary responsibility of all lifeguards is constant, vigilant surveillance, but this is no easy task for even the most experienced and professional lifeguards. Visual surveillance may be best described as close and continual observation of a person or group of people. Vigilance is defined as the watchfulness and wakefulness of paying close and continuous attention, but it is especially susceptible to fatigue.

Guarding against accidents and drowning through proactive prevention is the key to good lifeguarding. But to accomplish this in reality is indeed difficult. Visual surveillance is boring and tedious and requires a multitude of physical and psychological strategies to stay effective over time. Although lifeguarding texts often encourage constant vigilance as a lifeguarding requirement, truth be told, vigilance by humans is almost impossible to achieve. Humans are not good monitors. Computers are better monitors. However, lifeguarding is one of the few surveillance professions that is not assisted by technology. Lifeguards rely on their physical senses and skills to prevent injuries and drownings. As a result, lifeguards must call upon a variety of strategies and resources while watching the water rather than simply attempting to watch all the people in the water all the time.

Deteriorations in vigilance come early and often to those providing surveillance. For instance, vigilant surveillance becomes increasingly more difficult as temperature rises and as more people enter the water. These and other factors adversely affecting vigilant surveillance are discussed next in Psychology of Lifeguarding.

Psychology of Lifeguarding

Lifeguard training agencies give lifeguards the knowledge and water skills they need in order to do their jobs effectively. But there is also a great need for strategies to prevent boredom and keep lifeguards alert, particularly when they are on duty for long periods of time. Vigilance in general is difficult for all human beings but particularly difficult for teenagers, and most lifeguards in this country are teenagers. Lifeguard surveys continually indicate that boredom is a lifeguard's primary enemy. Although lifeguarding is an extremely important job and has many rewards, it can quickly become very tedious depending on the situation.

Although crowded days can be stressful for lifeguards, at least their attention typically increases with the size of the crowd. Most lifeguards would agree that slow days are more of a problem, at least from the standpoint of attention and con-

These lifeguards display active lifeguarding by situating themselves so one is standing on the beach and one is sitting up high. They display concentration and vigilance.

centration, than crowded days. On crowded days, however, more lifeguards are often necessary to visually cover the swimming area adequately.

Inverted-U Hypothesis

Since the early 1900s, much has been researched and written about the optimal level of psychological and emotional arousal for physical and mental tasks. In 1908, the Yerkes–Dodson law first illustrated how different levels of arousal predict performance. Basically stated, low levels of arousal and high levels of arousal lead to poor performance, while moderate levels of arousal lead to optimal performance in many endeavors. Low levels of arousal lead to poor performance through a lack of awareness and motivation, and high levels of arousal lead to panic and choking due to overloading, with potentially catastrophic results. Many areas including sports and medical training use the Yerkes–Dodson Law, sometimes referred to as the inverted-U hypothesis. Regardless of the sport or profession, to maximize performance, a little bit of nervousness or arousal is desirable. On the contrary, too much or too little arousal has a negative effect on performance. Lifeguards have known this for decades: Slow days and busy days produce either bored or overloaded lifeguards, and moderately busy days are best for attention, concentration, and awareness.

The field of medicine uses the Yerkes–Dodson Law to train physicians. Most medical schools use the motto "See one, do one, teach one." This refers to the competence and confidence levels of physicians performing vitally important medical procedures. Before being competent and confident in doing lifesaving procedures, particularly when time is of the essence, physicians should first see the procedure performed by another physician. Then after being further taught about the procedure, the physician may be ready to attempt the procedure on his own. However, the best medical educators truly believe that doctors become competent and confident in doing a procedure only after teaching it to other potential physicians. Lifeguards should be so lucky. Most often, the one and only time lifeguards perform a water rescue requiring resuscitation is their first and last. Lifeguards are expected, of course, to respond perfectly, professionally, and in a timely fashion, even though they have not had the opportunity to "see one, do one, teach one."

The Yerkes–Dodson law has important application for lifeguards. In essence, when lifeguards are busy and the weather is hot (overaroused), more lifeguards are needed for surveillance and to provide frequent rest breaks for the lifeguards on duty. To the contrary, when few patrons are in the water (underaroused), lifeguards on duty need to be challenged by their supervisors with "dummy drops," unannounced audits, staged water rescues, and anything else that can raise their arousal and attention. Because conditions at both surf beaches and water parks often lend themselves to real-life rescues by the on-duty lifeguards, boredom and low levels of arousal are not as common compared with traditional swimming pools and flat-water beaches. Although high levels of arousal may occur frequently for surf and water park lifeguards, low levels of arousal are more common for guards who are watching boring, rectangular, competitive swimming pools. Surf guards and water park lifeguards often have critical incidents, whereas pool lifeguards and flat-water lifeguards often do not. Regardless of the type of guarding environment, slow, monotonous days can lead to boredom and a lack of vigilance, whereas busy days can lead to overloading. To keep vigilance up for most lifeguards on most days, supervisors and managers must use tricks of the trade to keep their employees alert. Unfortunately, there has been insufficient research conducted specifically in the area of lifeguard surveillance, but research conducted in similar fields should apply to lifeguards today.

There are psychological and physiological strategies that lifeguards should utilize to decrease boredom and increase vigilance. Many athletes, pilots, and long-haul drivers already use these techniques effectively. More specifically, lifeguards should try to change positions or assignments at least every 30 minutes. In addition, moving frequently, mild exercise, working with a partner, cold water, and lowering ambient temperatures have proven to increase attention and concentration. Moderate increases in physical movement, respiration, and heart rate stimulate neurological pathways, which in turn improves attention, concentration, and vigilance. In short, research supports the view that an active and interactive lifeguard is more alert than a passive one. Lifeguards who continually sit rather than stand, walk, and otherwise move cannot maintain the same level of vigilance as those who are always in motion. The lifeguard who sits, stands, and strolls while on duty, as required by the five-minute scanning strategy (page 115), should be more alert physiologically and psychologically, provided she is well rested and not overly stimulated by other environmental factors.

Perceptual Body Blindness

For more than a quarter of a century, cognitive psychologists have been studying the phenomenon of perceptual blindness. Perceptual blindness can be simply explained as failing to detect the obvious in critical situations. Human beings are bad observers and poor monitors. We fail to see the most obvious things because although our eyes take in a tremendous amount of visual stimuli, very little of the data received by the eyes is actually encoded or recorded by our brains. Therefore we may see a lot but perceive very little, one reason humans are not infallible when it comes to drowning prevention and another reason why lifejackets are so important for nonswimmers. In essence, we as human beings see what we expect to see and what we want to see. That is why lifeguards and parents miss drowning victims: They don't want or expect people to actually drown and die on their watch. This happens on the subconscious level and may be described as perceptual body blindness. Although there are many forms and causes of perceptual blindness, the results are the same—drowning due to a lack of perception. Being aware of this concept and expecting the unexpected may help lifeguards and parents alike who are providing surveillance around the water.

Circadian Rhythms

Human beings, just like animals and plants, have biological clocks that predict levels of alertness and fatigue, with both levels fluctuating and alternating throughout each day. Unfortunately, peak times for alertness do not often coincide with the busiest times of the day at the beach. In general, people are most alert in the early to midmorning hours and again in the later afternoon. Between noon and the early afternoon, most people experience increased fatigue and reduced alertness. This is not comforting for those who supervise and manage beach lifeguards because these times of fatigue most often occur when the beaches are the most crowded. Figure 11.1 lists the Circadian Learning Center's nine switches of alertness.

Maturation and Motivation

As lifeguards become older and more experienced, they usually become more mature and motivated. Considering all lifeguards (pools, water parks, open water), their average age is very young. Lifeguards can begin working at many aquatic facilities at just 15 years of age, and studies conducted at Penn State University show that the average age of lifeguards in America is about 17. Surf lifeguards, however, in places such as Southern California and Florida, are of course much older than that, with many lifeguards being in their 20s and 30s. Remember that adolescence does not end until 25 years of age. The centers for judgment and decision making in the cerebral cortex do not completely form and mature until age 25. That is why many young adults still make bad decisions and exercise poor judgment. Even though some young teens are extremely mature beyond their years, adult decision making is not common until the mid-20s.

Hesitation and Indecision

Too often, lifeguards see or sense something out of the ordinary with a swimmer but continue to scan their zone of coverage with the intent of returning to double-check on the swimmer during the returning scan. This is particularly true for swimmers who are surface diving and swimming underwater. Not surprisingly, when lifeguards return their gaze to where the person was, she is no longer there. When this occurs at a beach, the victim is naturally much more difficult to find because of reduced water clarity and visibility. Waves and currents may also exacerbate the situation. The Ellis and Associates mantras "When you don't know, go!" and "When in doubt, check them out!" are so vitally important for drowning prevention. Likewise, if a lifeguard sees something at or beneath the surface of the water, he should investigate, even if it doesn't look exactly like a person; many drowning victims in the past have been mistaken for towels, shadows, or other inanimate objects and ignored by the lifeguard on duty. Lifeguards should not be racing into the water in an attempt to "save" everyone and everything, but contact should be made with every swimmer who raises a question in the guard's mind. This by definition is proactive prevention.

> ## FIGURE 11.1   Nine Switches of Alertness
>
> 1. **Interest, opportunity, a near miss, sense of danger:** Nothing is more awakening than a threat or danger, whether real or imagined. This is why unannounced audits and rescue drills are so highly recommended for keeping lifeguards alert and on their toes.
> 2. **Muscular activity:** Muscular activity, including walking, stretching, and standing, triggers the sympathetic nervous system, which helps keep people alert. Conversely, sitting with little movement suppresses the sympathetic nervous system, making it difficult to stay alert. The five-minute scanning strategy should help in this regard.
> 3. **Time of day or circadian clock:** Because the hours after lunch produce the lowest levels of arousal and alertness, this is when alertness switches should be used by lifeguards and supervisors to increase attention and concentration.
> 4. **Sleep bank balance:** Lack of sleep during the summer months, particularly for lifeguards in high school and college, is not uncommon and can create a sleep debt that can plummet people into dangerously low levels of daytime alertness. On a related note, a high percentage of lifeguards report to duty while hungover, as reported by *Aquatics International* magazine. Plenty of rest is required for lifeguard vigilance, but unfortunately this is difficult for management to control.
> 5. **Ingested food and chemicals:** Some ingested foods and chemicals temporarily increase alertness, whereas others induce drowsiness and inattentiveness, leading to sleep. Caffeine and certain energy drinks can increase alertness, while turkey, bananas, sleeping pills, medications, and others can induce sleepiness. Choosing the right substances to eat, drink, and ingest before and while on duty requires both research and good judgment on the part of the lifeguard and supervisor.
> 6. **Environmental light:** Bright light tends to increase alertness, while dim, subdued lighting leads to drowsiness. Cloudy, dreary days and nighttime guarding pose problems for lifeguard vigilance and should be addressed before going on duty.
> 7. **Temperature:** Cool, dry air, particularly on the face, helps keep people alert, whereas heat above 84 degrees Fahrenheit (28 °C) and humidity make people drowsy. This major concern for beach lifeguards must be dealt with appropriately by using fans, shade, hats, misting, and cold water. Going in the water frequently to cool off is highly recommended.
> 8. **Sound:** Constant sounds such as rolling waves breaking or the humming of machines can lead to drowsiness. On the other hand, intermittent sounds such as radios, voices, horns, bells, and whistles can increase alertness. Although for years lifeguards were not allowed to talk while on duty, today's lifeguards are encouraged to talk, provided they do not engage in prolonged conversation or take their eyes off the water.
> 9. **Aroma:** Some smells such as peppermint can promote alertness, while others such as lavender can promote drowsiness and sleep.
>
> Adapted, by permission, from CIRCADIAN®.

Strategies for Improving Vigilance and Emergency Response

Lifeguards agree that boredom while on duty is their enemy. This section presents strategies for reducing boredom while increasing attention and concentration. Boredom and distractions lead to human error, the leading cause of accidents worldwide.

The Five-Minute Scanning Strategy

The five-minute scanning strategy is a system developed to improve lifeguard alertness, concentration, and vigilance. The technique is based on the psychological aspects of lifeguarding discussed earlier in the chapter and on approximately five years of data accumulated and analyzed at three major universities (Penn State University, University of Maryland, and East Carolina University). More than 10,000 lifeguards were surveyed throughout North America to see how they stayed alert while on duty, and their responses were combined with other research on vigilance collected since World War II in a variety of areas. The five-minute scanning strategy was developed in the late 1990s and has become popular with many swimming pool and particularly water park guards throughout the United States and some other countries. The strategy may prove even more beneficial for open-water lifeguards because, in general, they tend to remain stationed at the same post for long periods of time since it is not as easy to rotate stations for open-water lifeguards, especially surf lifeguards.

Simply stated, the five-minute scanning strategy is an arousal and safety check every five minutes that helps keep on-duty lifeguards active, alert, and vigilant. It is highly recommended for anyone providing visual surveillance of others. This strategy is very flexible and easy, simply calling for eye, body, and mind changes every five minutes. While on duty, a lifeguard should change the following elements:

- Position
- Pattern (eye)
- Posture
- People (count)

In the five-minute scanning strategy, the lifeguard attempts to change as many of these four components as possible every five minutes. If guarding from the center position of the lifeguard station, after five minutes, the lifeguard should move to the left or right of the station and scan from that perspective. If sweeping the eyes from left to right while scanning, the lifeguard should change the eye pattern to a circular eye pattern or an up and down sweeping scan. If sitting, the lifeguard should change to standing and vice versa. Finally, particularly when the swimming area is not too crowded, the lifeguard should attempt to quickly count the people in her zone of coverage. When large crowds are in the water, however, lifeguards simply need to group or cluster those in their zones.

A simple way to remember the most important keys of this scanning strategy is to sit, stand, and stroll every five minutes, keeping in mind that the stroll, or foot patrol, must keep the lifeguard

in full view of the water and should not be performed when an overcrowded shoreline obstructs the lifeguard's view. This strategy becomes easier as the size of the lifeguard station becomes larger. If the lifeguard station has indoor and outdoor segments and a ramp to the beach, the entire station can be utilized for the five-minute scan.

Another suggestion for lifeguards with unusually large or active swimmers in their zones is to quickly mentally rehearse how they would rescue a difficult person should he become distressed in the water. Knowing how to effect the rescue, what equipment would be used, and who would be summoned for assistance beforehand is always of great value. Using the five-minute scanning strategy not only helps keep lifeguards more alert but also makes the day go faster. When the strategy is required by lifeguards on duty, they are also more easily supervised because a beach manager or head lifeguard can simply watch the lifeguards to see if they make significant changes every five minutes. Finally, the public at the beach will certainly notice how much more alert the lifeguards appear to be because they are not just sitting for extended periods of time in the same location.

This lifeguard is appropriately dressed and positioned as she patrols the dock in a large flat-water lake.

The 5/30 Model of Aquatic Accountability

Going hand in hand with the five-minute scanning strategy is the 30-minute supervisory check. Once lifeguards are required to do the five-minute scan, supervisors and managers can then check on the lifeguards and the beach every 30 minutes, if possible. When checking on the lifeguards, a comprehensive evaluation is not necessary; a simple quick check of the guards as to their position, wearing uniforms, alertness, and active scanning process is sufficient. During this 30-minute check, being a "good cop" is preferred so that a positive relationship between the lifeguard and the supervisor can be established. Checking to see if the lifeguard on duty has an adequate supply of cold water, shade, sunscreen, equipment, and other important lifeguarding items can greatly enhance the lifeguard's performance as well as foster a good association between lifeguard and administration. Some aquatic administrators have claimed that when the five-minute scanning strategy is coupled with the 5/30 aquatic accounting model, in-water rescues are significantly reduced.

STARR Method for Responding to Aquatic Emergencies

Adapted, by permission, from *American Lifeguard Magazine*, 2002.

The STARR method was developed by Kim W. Tyson and Robert E. Ogoreuc. The purpose of STARR is to provide lifeguard instructors, training officers, and lifeguards with a basic tool to use when educating lifeguards in the methods and techniques for responding to aquatic emergencies. The acronym STARR was developed to assist lifeguards in performing key elements of an aquatic rescue. STARR stands for scan, target, assess, rescue, and removal of a victim of an aquatic emergency.

Scan

Using preventive lifeguarding techniques, the lifeguards on duty should be vigilant and observant of the water they are watching. During the scanning phase a lifeguard will select the best observation techniques, specific to the design of the facility, location of the lifeguard, location of the lifeguard chairs, number of swimmers, activity of the swimmers, their swimming ability, and the changing environmental conditions the lifeguard is faced with.

While the lifeguards are scanning their water zones, they should constantly be evaluating the swimmers' ability, the swimmers' activities, and changing water conditions. This evaluation process will help lifeguards determine which patrons are at higher risk than others. The lifeguards can now target people who may be in need of preventive actions and possible rescue procedures.

Target

The targeting phase can best be described as locking onto people who are entering hazardous conditions or exhibiting signs of fatigue, panic, distress, and potentially the instinctive drowning response (IDR). A person exhibiting the IDR is unable to call out for help, has instinctive arm movements (arms paddling below the surface), and has no supporting kick (Pia 1991). The IDR can last 20 to 60 seconds (Pia 1991). Distressed swimmers will need to be signaled, alerted, and waved into shallower water; prohibited from engaging in the activity they are performing; or possibly removed from the water if conditions and skill level warrant. If the swimmer does not react or is nonresponsive, the lifeguard must quickly initiate the preplanned emergency action plan for responding to this aquatic emergency. If the targeted person is in need of assistance, then the lifeguard must activate the emergency action plan by blowing her whistle or using another communication device (radio or phone), leave her station, and quickly approach the victim. As the lifeguard is approaching, she needs to keep the victim in sight and assess the victim's changing behavioral conditions as well as the environmental conditions.

Assess

Assessment begins from the moment the lifeguard is on duty and starts to watch his water. During this phase of STARR, the lifeguard focuses on assessing the people in his zone while targeting and locking onto any potential victims. Once a lifeguard recognizes the signs of a distressed swimmer or a potential drowning situation, he needs to choose the appropriate rescue equipment and the best method to approach the victim, maintain visual contact, watch for behavioral changes in the victim, make contact, and take control of the victim (Brewster 1995). This is often referred to as integrated problem solving, in which the rescuer evaluates the scene and the person's behavior as well as any changing conditions that would cause the rescuer to modify the rescue sequence and events.

Rescue

Rescue is the point where contact with, control of, and support of the victim take place. The lifeguard should attempt to keep the rescue flotation device (rescue can, tube, buoy) between herself and the victim to maximize his safety and support. The lifeguard should try to verbally calm the victim and provide the best stabilization that will provide both air and support. The rescuer needs to identify herself to the victim, telling him she is a trained lifeguard and reassuring him that the situation is under control. Once the victim is stabilized, the rescuer should then determine how she should transport and remove the victim from the water. The rescuer will have to determine if she needs additional lifeguards to assist in the rescue and removal as well as the best route of extraction. If additional help is needed, she uses the appropriate hand, whistle, or buoy equipment signal to activate additional rescuers in the water. Choosing the best route for extraction requires evaluating the water and surf conditions such as wind, waves, rip currents, density of swimmer load, lateral currents, shoreline obstructions, inshore holes, and drop-offs.

Removal

Removal is the last point of the STARR method. The lifeguard should react to changing water conditions and control the victim while swimming into shore and watching for incoming waves. If waves are present, the rescuer should let the victim know when waves are incoming and then secure the victim. The victim needs to be taken to shallow water where she can stand and be transported out of the water. If the victim cannot stand and walk, rescuers must provide additional assistance by carrying the victim out of the water and positioning her on the beach for first aid and life support care, unless spinal cord injury is suspected. In the case of spinal cord injury, lifeguards should follow their agency's standard operating procedures for suspected spinal injuries. Once on the beach, the victim should be monitored for vital signs; information should be collected and recorded detailing the rescue and condition of the victim. In life-threatening situations, more advanced medical care is needed and should be summoned immediately. A debriefing should occur among supervisors and lifeguards to evaluate the rescue. Record the date and vital information, and ensure that all rescuers are prepared mentally and physically to return to duty.

STARR's intent is to give lifeguards a tool that will allow them to apply problem-solving skills when lifeguarding and responding to aquatic emergencies.

Systematic Observation Skills and Shadow Guarding

Adapted, by permission, from B. McKinley and R.E. Ogoreuc, 2005, *American Lifeguard Magazine*.

Direct systematic observation is a valuable tool for training new teachers to collect data regarding the educational environment. Information gained from analysis of systematic observation data is useful in helping preservice teachers make informed, correct decisions regarding many aspects of teaching (Rink 1998).

The same observation skill training is vital when training lifeguards. Learning and applying systematic observation skills is a responsibility of all rookie lifeguards. Unless a lifeguard can systematically scan, observe, and make timely and correct decisions based on his observations, valuable rescue time can be lost (Ellis and Associates 1999; American Red Cross 2001; Brewster 2003; White 2006). Learning the importance of observation skills during lifeguard training is basic. However, knowing and understanding how to scan, what to look for during the scan, and the protocols to follow throughout a scan are far different skills than actually performing an observation (YMCA of the USA 2001). It is not uncommon for different people, watching the same event, to have far differing perceptions of what occurred (Darst, Zakrajsek, and Mancini 1989). Using systematic observation during lifeguard training helps rookies understand the specific criteria to look for and adds a point of reference from which reflections and further practice can evolve. Taking subjective perceptions out of each observation, and replacing perceptions with actual documentation of what the lifeguard observed, is a critical skill for all lifeguards to master.

Agencies certifying lifeguards generally agree on numerous discrete skills needed to master the requirements of a certified lifeguard. Beyond actual rescue protocols and aquatic expertise, related skills include checking equipment, scanning beaches and waterfronts, determining beach and wave conditions, interacting with patrons, properly timing scans, and using emergency rescue equipment as well as knowing methods of leaving the lifeguard station, backup protocols, and emergency rescue responsibilities (Ellis and Associates 1999; American Red Cross 2001; YMCA of the USA 2001; Brewster 2003). Although keen observation is a necessary and critical responsibility of all lifeguards, using observation skills to apply systematic observation to numerous areas simultaneously is a skill that needs to be practiced by rookie lifeguards.

Shadow guarding is not formally mentioned in lifeguarding literature. However, some organizations informally refer to shadow guarding; it is a method of placing rookie lifeguards in real-world situations so they can spend time at an aquatic facility and observe senior lifeguards at work (Boyce 2000). Although informal observations can certainly offer a new and different perspective from participation in a structured class or lecture format, unless specific criteria are established for the rookie to look for and document, the shadow experience may not be as beneficial as intended.

A predetermined set of criteria, in the form of written cues, for the person shadowing (and the person in charge of training) may create a more focused learning experience and reinforce necessary skills.

The use of formal documentation can assist rookie lifeguards as they learn the many responsibilities associated with observation skills. Lifeguards are responsible for observing many areas. Crowds, watercraft, jetties, weather, beach conditions, and surf conditions are some of the areas that lifeguards need to consistently address.

To determine the varied responsibilities involved in observing delineated waterfront areas, the shadow guard grid (SGG) was piloted during the summer of 2004 at Ocean City, New Jersey. The accompanying criteria were determined as a result of the pilot study. However, the grid can be amended to suit the needs of specific aquatic facilities (pools, water parks, beaches).

Lifeguards shadowing on the Jersey Shore. The more experienced guard points out "hot spots" and other concerns for the rookie lifeguard.

Although a useful tool at any stage of lifeguard training, the grid is particularly helpful after initial practice in the classroom with a video of a waterfront facility. In the classroom setting, the instructor can carefully monitor use of the grid and offer specific and task-appropriate feedback to rookies. The second step involves using the grid at a waterfront facility, followed by senior lifeguard reflection with the rookie focusing on the grid documentation.

The SGG can be adapted to any lifeguard training situation. Categories for facility conditions, number of lifeguards observed, and specific duties can be amended to replicate the real-world setting of any waterfront. And finally, the SGG can be used as a companion to in-class activities, where rookie lifeguards can all watch a film, scan the same video, and then with instructor input analyze their responses as a group.

An additional benefit of the SGG is the reflection tool for both rookie and senior lifeguards. The SGG serves as a written documentation focusing on what was observed, thereby permitting collaboration between rookies and senior guards. Further, reliability in observations (interrater reliability) can be determined by comparing consistency of observations among lifeguards at differing levels of expertise while observing the same situations using the same criteria. And finally, the SGG can assist both rookie and senior lifeguards in pointing out areas of omission in observation that need to be brought to their attention.

Using the SGG as a means of training rookie lifeguards, or as a means of staying current with requirements for senior lifeguards, is a strategy that can only increase skills and shorten response time. This process provides lifeguard instructors with feedback regarding their effectiveness as teachers and gives rookies a measure of their success and progress in learning new skills.

Summary

To be the best they can be, lifeguards should know and use all the lifeguarding and lifesaving techniques advocated by all the water safety agencies. What is offered here is newer, vitally important information that supplements what is learned in lifeguard certification programs. To ensure you understand all the proactive preventive lifeguarding techniques, read all the lifeguard manuals available from each training agency.

12

United States Lifesaving Association and International Life Saving Federation

B. Chris Brewster
United States Lifesaving Association and International Life Saving Federation

Particularly when it comes to setting standards for lifeguarding open-water areas with waves and currents, nobody does it better than the United States Lifesaving Association (USLA) and the International Life Saving Federation (ILS). But these organizations do not deal solely with surf beaches; they also have much to offer those running flat-water beaches, river beaches, and other open-water areas. The ILS goes further, including pools and water parks as well. The professionalism exuded by both organizations is a model for others to follow.

The United States Lifesaving Association (www.usla.org) is America's nonprofit professional association of beach lifeguards and open-water rescuers. In existence since 1964, the USLA aims primarily to reduce death and injury in the aquatic environment through various strategies, including educating the public, setting and disseminating lifeguard standards, offering training programs, promoting high levels of lifeguard preparedness, and conducting lifeguard competitions. This chapter provides the goals and objectives as well as the historical development of both the USLA and ILS. Emulating USLA and ILS standards will increase the professionalism of your staff.

History of the United States Lifesaving Association

Professional beach lifeguarding in the United States began in the 1890s as beach resorts were constructed along the east coast. It evolved locally, at venues throughout the United States, as interest in open-water swimming grew and deaths due to drowning occurred. For decades, the United States had no common training standard for open-water lifeguards, with each lifeguard agency setting its own. In contrast, for example, Australia approached lifesaving quite differently. Although lifesaving there began later, in 1907, and was a volunteer system, it was overseen from the start by a regional body that eventually became the national organization known as Surf Life Saving Australia. So rather than local control, there was national oversight, and rather than paid lifeguards, there were volunteer lifesavers.

There was little communication between America's professional lifeguards and Australia's volunteer lifesavers until Australia was chosen to host the 1956 Summer Olympics. On that occasion, the volunteer lifesavers of Australia decided to conduct an international invitational competition, inviting lifesavers (including lifeguards) from several countries, and asking only that the teams be selected by each nation's national body. There was no such body in the United States, and since Australia's invitation was received by California lifeguards, they organized a team under the banner of the Surf Life Saving Association of America (SLSA) even though they were solely from two agencies: Los Angeles County and Los Angeles City.

The Australian event drew a crowd of 115,000 spectators, with the legendary "Duke" Paoa Kahanamoku of Hawaii as the honorary chairman. It was a great success, allowing participants to share their knowledge of different lifesaving equipment and forming bonds that were to be invaluable in coming years.

After the event, Los Angeles County lifeguard chief Bud Stevenson decided to use SLSA in his efforts to upgrade professional lifeguarding, and it became, for a time, the political arm of the Los Angeles County lifeguards. This allowed for apparently independent political action that was outwardly separate from that of the managers of the lifeguard service. Chief Stevenson appointed one of his lifeguards, Bob Burnside, who had been a member of the competition team, as president of the new organization.

In 1963, Burnside called for a meeting of lifeguards from lifesaving agencies throughout Southern California in an effort to broaden the reach of the organization. The year 1964 is viewed as the birth of the United States Lifesaving Association, when representatives from various California surf lifeguard agencies agreed to its formation, calling it the National Surf Life Saving Association (NSLSA). This lofty name aside, it was not until 1979 that the organization broadened to truly encompass all of the United States, to include beach lifeguards at lakes as members, and to become known as the United States Lifesaving Association.

Impact of the USLA on American Lifesaving

Over the years, perhaps the greatest contribution of the USLA to American lifeguarding has been to act as a catalyst for sharing of information among lifeguard agencies, both nationally and internationally. Like other public safety providers, lifeguards tended to be insular, clinging to methods developed locally. In the absence of national standards, this approach continued unabated until lifeguards began communicating with one another, often through the USLA, and reviewing methods developed by their peers.

A dream of the founders of the USLA was to create national standards, where none existed, under the presumption that not every approach to lifesaving could be the best and that by identifying the best practices, all lifesaving would benefit. A key step was a national conference in 1980 at Texas A&M University in Galveston. The purpose was to develop guidelines for establishing open-water recreational beach standards. The conference was cosponsored by the USLA, the American Camping Association, and the Council for National Cooperation in Aquatics. The outcome set a foundation for what national experts believed minimum standards for beach lifeguarding should include. (The document is available in the Lifeguard Library section of www.usla.org.)

From this base, the USLA developed specific recommended standards for the training of beach lifeguards, including a minimum age (16), equipment they should have available, and basic skills they would need to meet and maintain. Unlike other organizations training lifeguards, the USLA decided to let lifeguard agencies (mostly public employers) continue to conduct training and to certify (essentially accredit) agencies that chose to apply and could show they were in compliance with the recommended standards. Today, more than 100 lifeguard agencies are certified as conducting their operations in accordance with these standards. Be sure to review the specific standards for your region, as they differ between geographic locations.

The USLA has long emphasized the proactive value of drowning prevention versus the reactive value of rescue. The association estimates that for every rescue from drowning performed by a beach lifeguard, well over 100 preventive actions are taken. These range from advising beachgoers of areas to avoid, moving people out of hazardous areas (at surf beaches most typically because of rip currents), and enforcing beach regulations that may reduce the chance of accidents. Comprehensive prevention also involves public education, long before beachgoers arrive at beach areas.

The USLA is composed of individual members, most of whom are professional lifeguards, affiliated in local chapters. These chapters form the regions of the USLA, and delegates from the regions appoint the national leadership. Much of the public education work of the association is provided locally. Chapters and regions conduct events such as community lectures and school assemblies. They disseminate safety materials developed locally and by the USLA nationally. The USLA itself distributes safety information most broadly through its website at www.usla .org, the news media, brochures, signs, and various publications.

Junior lifeguard programs, which are youth programs similar to summer camps but with a lifesaving focus, were first initiated by beach lifeguard agencies in the United States. These programs have thrived, partly with the support of the USLA and a sharing of information through USLA contacts. Today, more than half the membership of the USLA is composed of junior lifeguards. In other countries, various similar programs have been developed as well.

Over the years, the USLA has joined with other national organizations to leverage its expertise and broaden its reach. One of its more successful efforts has involved an alliance with the U.S. government's National Oceanic and Atmospheric Administration, including Sea Grant and the National Weather Service, to create a national education program on rip currents, the cause of more than 80 percent of rescues at surf beaches. Educational websites, signs, and brochures have resulted.

Although the USLA does not directly train or certify individual lifeguards, leaving this up to affiliated lifesaving agencies, it does produce a standardized curriculum and various training materials that are followed nationwide. These include *Open Water Lifesaving: The United States Lifesaving Association Manual* (Brewster 2003), along with educational DVDs and other tools for instructors.

Advocacy is an important role of the USLA. In areas where drowning deaths are high, because of the absence or lack of lifeguards, the USLA has taken a high profile in recommending the provision of lifeguards or the enhancement of existing programs. A Centers for Disease Control and Prevention document, *Lifeguard Effectiveness*, has profiled a number of successful efforts by the USLA that have resulted in the initiation of lifesaving programs that prevent scores of drowning deaths each year, where once they were common.

Lifeguard competitions were introduced by the USLA, and they continue to be an important aspect of USLA programs. Through competitions, organized locally, regionally, and nationally, the USLA promotes the high levels of fitness required in the profession, in which the physical capabilities of the rescuer are a determining factor in the success of each rescue. Competitions also demonstrate the value of lifesaving to the public and further the sharing of ideas among lifeguards.

From a policy perspective, it has been said that if a rescue from drowning isn't recorded, it

These junior lifeguards provide extra surveillance as well as buoyant rescue crafts for long-distance open swims.

didn't happen. That may not be literally true, but justifying the cost of public safety services has long required demonstrating the frequency with which it is called on and its success. Thus police and fire departments are able to produce statistics that sometimes seem to rival those of professional sports. Lifesaving has the same needs.

For more than 25 years, the USLA has annually solicited statistics on lifeguard activities. These statistics, regularly cited by the news media and used in the development of lifesaving policies, are submitted by individual lifeguard agencies. They are available at www.usla.org. Figure 12.1 lists annual averages reported by an average of 96 lifeguard agencies from throughout the United States during the most recently available five-year period.

The chance that a person will die by drowning while attending a beach protected by USLA-

affiliated lifeguards is 1 in 18 million (.0000056 percent). This is based on 10 years of reports from USLA-affiliated lifeguard agencies, comparing estimated beach attendance to the number of drowning deaths in areas under lifeguard protection.

Through these and many other efforts, the USLA, a 501(c)3 charitable, nonprofit organization, continues to have a major impact on ensuring the safety of America's beaches. Without it, the growth and professionalism of beach lifesaving would be nowhere near what we see today. As the Centers for Disease Control and Prevention has stated in its report *Lifeguard Effectiveness*, "Most drownings are preventable through a variety of strategies, one of which is to provide lifeguards in public areas where people are known to swim and to encourage people to swim in those protected areas." The USLA works to ensure that lifeguards

FIGURE 12.1   Statistics on Lifeguard Activities in 2009

312,676,724 beach visits (daily attendance)

82,998 rescues from drowning

6,457,403 preventive actions (to prevent accidents)

265,357 medical aids

3,319 boat rescues

7,425 boat passengers rescued

$82,396,415 (estimated value of boats rescued)

124 total drowning deaths in reporting agency jurisdictions

103 drowning deaths in unguarded (unstaffed) areas

21 drowning deaths in guarded (staffed) areas

15,143 lost and found people (usually children)

10,750 public safety lectures

293,514 attendees at public safety lectures

Adapted, by permission, from United States Lifeguard Association 2009.

are in place, trained, and equipped to appropriate levels to prevent most drownings and other aquatic accidents.

Although the professional category of USLA membership is open only to professional open-water rescuers, anyone can be a member of the association through other membership categories, such as associate member. Since membership is the primary source of support of the organization, everyone is encouraged to join and thereby support the USLA.

International Life Saving Federation

For more than a century, the ILS has been functioning in a fashion similar to the USLA. The ILS enjoys the cooperation of many countries internationally.

Beginnings of a Global Lifesaving Organization

In 1910, representatives from Belgium, Denmark, France, Great Britain, Luxembourg, and Switzerland gathered in Paris, France, and agreed to create an international lifesaving organization called Fédération Internationale de Sauvetage (International Life Saving Federation). Spain and Italy, which were not present, also agreed to participate.

The two world wars interrupted progress, but in 1952, the constitution of the organization was updated and it was reborn. It operated under several different names until 1985, when it became known as Fédération Internationale de Sauvetage Aquatique (International Aquatic Life Saving Federation). It ultimately came to include more than 30 full-member national lifesaving organizations. The primary focus was pool and lake lifesaving, and the greatest concentration of membership was in Europe.

Separately, in 1971, five national surf-oriented lifesaving organizations from Australia, Great Britain, New Zealand, South Africa, and the United States agreed to form World Life Saving (WLS). The United States Lifesaving Association was the founding member from the United States. Over the years, WLS came to include more than 20 full-member national lifesaving organizations. The primary focus of the WLS was surf lifesaving.

Both organizations provided a wide variety of services to lifesaving. They served as agents for the international exchange of ideas about best practices in lifesaving, sponsored international conferences and exhibitions, conducted competitions, and generally promoted the discipline of lifesaving and drowning prevention. As a result of their work, innovations in one area of the world were shared so that good ideas could be adopted by all. This of course increased safety at the aquatic areas under protection.

Recognizing the value of each organization, but concluding that they would be better as one, leaders of the organizations discussed the possibility of a merger. In 1994, the two international organizations coalesced into a single worldwide lifesaving organization called the International Life Saving Federation (www.ilsf.org), which has served the global lifesaving community and the cause of drowning prevention since that time.

ILS Composition and Strategies

The ILS is a nonpolitical, nonreligious, humanitarian organization. It is the world authority in the global effort to prevent drowning. It accomplishes its goals by leading, supporting, and partnering with national and international organizations committed to drowning prevention, aquatic safety supervision, emergency response, and lifesaving sport.

There are three categories of membership in the ILS, each requiring that the member be a nonprofit organization: full member (one per country), associate member (two per country), and corresponding member (unlimited number per country). As a founding member of the ILS, the United States Lifesaving Association is the full member from the United States. In 1996, the YMCA of the USA became an associate member, and in 1998, the American Red Cross became an associate member.

The ILS is led by a globally elected president and secretary general. It is divided, politically, into four regions of the world: Africa, Americas, Asia Oceania, and Europe. These regions, which are responsible for the development and support of lifesaving organizations in their areas, elect their own presidents, who simultaneously serve as the four vice presidents of the ILS. They also elect delegates to the ILS board of directors.

The ILS has created commissions composed of various committees and working groups responsible for the management, development, and technical aspects of each major ILS field of activity. All members of these groups and of the board of directors are unpaid volunteers. The ILS also cooperates with partner organizations, governments, nongovernment organizations (NGOs), and sponsors to promote lifesaving worldwide. For example, the ILS is formally recognized by the International Committee of the Red Cross and the International Olympic Committee and works closely with the World Health Organization.

The ILS has set out a number of specific key goals in its constitution, including the following:

• Seeking the best methods and means of aquatic lifesaving, drowning prevention, resuscitation of the apparently drowned, and emergency care

• Teaching lifesaving and establishing educational exchanges of aquatic lifesaving techniques and operations

• Exchanging practical, medical, and scientific experiences in the field of aquatic lifesaving and drowning prevention

• Extending the activities of the ILS to all places throughout the world and communicating and cooperating with other international humanitarian bodies

• Promoting uniformity concerning equipment, information, symbols, and laws for control and regulation within the aquatic environment

• Promoting and organizing lifesaving sports in order to stimulate the ability and willingness of lifesavers

• Encouraging the convening of international lifesaving congresses

Although financial resources of the ILS are limited, the strength of the organization lies in its members and their willingness to share and support lifesaving activities. A key method through which the ILS helps prevent drowning is by promoting the development of national lifesaving organizations in countries without them and then supporting those organizations so they can provide and support lifesaving activities. The ILS also regularly convenes international conferences, identifies best practices, evaluates drowning prevention methods and drowning-related medical procedures, issues policy statements on its findings, and works closely with like-minded international organizations.

Summary

Aquatic lifesaving is a relatively new discipline, when compared to other public safety professions like firefighting or law enforcement, that has emerged historically only in the past several hundred years. Around the world, lifesaving efforts began locally, regionally, and nationally. Many lifesavers and lifesaving organizations worked independently, unaware of the innovations of others and unable to share their own innovations. In fact, there are many interesting methods of lifesaving, but only a few of them can be considered best practices. Through the International Life Saving Federation and its member associations, approaches to lifesaving are carefully reviewed, and the best approaches are ultimately identified for the good of lifesavers throughout the world and the people they seek to protect.

Appendix A

Cost–Benefit Analysis Matrix for Nonswimming Alternatives

Method name	Initial costs	Annual costs	Potential effectiveness (high, medium, low)	Aesthetic and user impacts (negative, positive, neutral)	Total ranking

From T. Griffiths, 2011, *Safer beaches* (Champaign, IL: Human Kinetics).

Appendix B

Lifeguard Observation Event Recording

Observer: _____ Date: _____

Guard: _____ Location: _____

Water conditions: _____ Number of patrons: _____

Weather conditions: _____

Purpose: The rookie lifeguard gains valuable experience and insight regarding the responsibilities of lifeguarding by observing guards on duty, patrons in the area, and the immediate environment. This 30-second event recording form will document rookie lifeguard observations in a real-world environment.

Instructions: For a 60-minute time period, place a hash mark every 30 seconds in the area that corresponds with what each lifeguard is doing at that specific time.

Guard interaction or position	Guard 1 Position:	Guard 2 Position:	Guard 3 Position:
Guard location (Lifeguard stand or tower, boat, paddleboard, in water with rescue can)	Total box =	Total box =	Total box =
Watching the water (Actively scanning: moving the head)	Total box =	Total box =	Total box =
Public education Speaking with patron (giving directions, verbal feedback)	Total box =	Total box =	Total box =
Preventive actions (Directing to shallow water, stopping horseplay or diving, etc.)	Total box =	Total box =	Total box =
First aid (Land based)	Total box =	Total box =	Total box =
Water rescue (Actively involved in a water rescue)	Total box =	Total box =	Total box =

(continued)

From T. Griffiths, 2011, *Safer beaches* (Champaign, IL: Human Kinetics).

(continued)

Calculation Totals

Guard location   Total box marks for all guards = _____

Watching the water   Total box marks for all guards = _____

Public education   Total box marks for all guards = _____

Preventive actions   Total box marks for all guards = _____

First aid (land based)   Total box marks for all guards = _____

Water rescue   Total box marks for all guards = _____

                                     Total marks for all boxes = _____

Calculating Your Data

1. Add the total marks for each box separately, and place in box.
2. Add the total marks for all boxes in all rows.
3. Divide the total for all boxes in all rows into the total marks for each separate box—this will give you a percentage of interactions or performance for each separate lifeguard, in each specified observation category.

Example: Preventive Actions Observations

Preventive actions (guard 1):   Total marks in guard 1's box = 23

Sum of all marks in all boxes = 175

Divide 23 (total marks in guard 1's box) by 175 (total in all boxes) = 13%

Example of Interpretation for Written Report, Referring to the Correctives Block for Lifeguard 1

Preventive actions block: Lifeguard observation data in the preventive actions block were recorded as follows: Lifeguard 1 gave 23 correctives to patrons during the observation period. Thirteen percent of all lifeguard feedback was in the form of preventive actions. The reason for the lifeguard feedback ratios in this category may have been due to the following: _____

_____.

Note: Guard interpretation must be strictly documented according to actual recorded data for each category. Interpretation must clearly mirror the data collected and the duties delineated in each category.

References and Resources

American National Standards Institute. (2007). *ANSI Z535.2:2007 Environmental and facility safety signs*. New York: ANSI.

American Red Cross. (2001). *Lifeguard training*. San Bruno, CA: StayWell.

Black, D.E., Donnelley, L.P., and Settle, R.F. (1990). Equitable arrangements for financing beach nourishment projects. *Ocean & Shoreline Management* 14: 191-214.

Boyce, J. (2000). Arlington aquatic centers introduce lifeguarding program for youth. Arlington Public Schools website.

Brewster, C. (Ed.). (1995). *The United States Lifesaving Association manual of open water lifesaving*. Englewood Cliffs, NJ: Brady.

Brewster, C. (Ed.). (2003). *Open water lifesaving: The United States Lifesaving Association manual* (2nd ed.). Boston: Pearson.

California Coastal Commission. (1997). *California coastal guide*. Berkeley: University of California Press.

City of South Haven. (2010). Beach and pier safety. Available: www.south-haven.com/pages/beaches /Beach_Pier_Safety_Book.pdf.

Crompton, J.L. (1999). *Financing and acquiring park and recreation resources*. Champaign, IL: Human Kinetics.

Darst, P., Zakrajsek, D., and Mancini, V. (Eds.). (1989). *Analyzing physical education and sport instruction* (2nd ed.). Champaign, IL: Human Kinetics.

Douglass, S.L. (2002). *Saving America's beaches: The causes of and solutions to beach erosion*. Singapore: World Scientific Publishing.

Ellis and Associates. (1999). *National pool and waterpark lifeguard training* (2nd ed.). Toronto: Jones and Bartlett.

Grand Haven Pier Safety Task Force. (1996). A matter of life and death. Brochure produced by TV5 as a service to the Grand Haven Public Schools. Detroit District, Army Corps of Engineers.

Grand Haven Pier Safety Task Force. (1996). A matter of life and death. Video produced by TV5 as a service to the Grand Haven Public Schools. Detroit District, Army Corps of Engineers.

Great Lakes Beach and Pier Safety Task Force. (n.d.). Respect the power. Available: www.respectthepower .org/index.html.

Griffiths, T. (1999). *Better beaches*. Ashburn, VA: National Recreation and Park Association.

Griffiths, T. (2003). *The complete swimming pool reference*. Champaign, IL: Sagamore.

Gunter, V.J., Ditton, R.B., and Olson, S.G. (1987). An assessment of beach access and management issues on Galveston Island. *Coastal Management* 15: 247-260.

International Organization for Standardization. (2008). *ISO 20712-1. Water safety signs and beach safety flags. Part 1. Specifications for water safety signs used in workplaces and public areas*. Geneva: ISO.

Keshler, B. (1999). "Drowning Intervention: An Army Corps of Engineers Perspective," *Drowning: New Perspectives on Intervention and Prevention*. Boca Raton, FL: CRC Press, pp. 165-176.

Markel Insurance Company. *Risk management for your aquatic safety program*. Glen Allen, VA: Markel Insurance Company.

National Oceanic and Atmospheric Administration, Coastal Services Center. (n.d.). Beach nourishment: A guide for local government officials. Available: www.csc.noaa.gov/beachnourishment/html/human /socio/shares.htm.

North Carolina Department of Environment and Natural Resources. (2008). Public beach and waterfront access: Grant program for local governments. Available: http://dcm2.enr.state.nc.us/access/grants.htm.

Ocean and Coastal Resource Management. (n.d.). The Coastal and Estuarine Land Conservation Program. Available: http://coastalmanagement.noaa.gov/land /welcome.html.

Pia, F. (1991). Reducing swimming related drowning fatalities. *Pennsylvania Recreation and Parks* Spring: 13-16.

Ravella, P.A. (2008). Beach project financing. Available: www.townofnagshead.net/index.asp.

Rink, J. (1998). *Teaching physical education for learning* (2nd ed.). Boston: McGraw-Hill.

Salmon Restoration Association. (n.d.). Available: www.salmonrestoration.com/home.html.

Scheder, C. (2010). *Camp waterfront management*. Monterey, CA: American Camping Association.

Sharockman, A., and Van Sant, W. (2008, June 11). Rays seek Pinellas hotel tax extension for ballpark. *St. Petersburg Times*. Available: www.tampabay.com /news/localgovernment/article617217.ece.

TCoast Talk. (2009). Martin County considers parking fees at beaches, boat ramps. Available: www .tcoasttalk.com/2009/03/11/martin-county-considers-parking-fees-at-beaches-boat-ramps.

Trust for Public Land. (2005). American beach properties preserved. Available: www.tpl.org/tier3_print.cfm?folder_id=250&content_item_id=20022&mod_type=1.

US News and World Report. (2008, January). 50 Ways to Improve Your Life.

Walton Sun. (2009, July 24). $4 million federal grant to help pay for Miramar beach repairs in Walton County. Available: www.waltonsun.com/articles/washington-3354-million-beach.html.

White, J.E. (2006). *StarGuard: Best practices for lifeguards* (3rd ed.). Champaign, IL: Human Kinetics.

YMCA of the USA. (2001). *On the guard II: The YMCA lifeguard manual* (4th ed.). Champaign, IL: Human Kinetics.

Yoder, D.G., and Ham, L.L. (2005). Partnerships. In B. van der Smissen, M. Moiseichik, and V.J. Hartenburg, (Eds.), *Management of park and recreation agencies* (2nd ed.), pp. 85-101. Ashburn, VA: National Recreation and Park Association.

Index

Note: The letters *f* and *t* after page numbers indicate figures and tables, respectively.

About the Author

Tom Griffiths, EdD, has over 40 years of experience in aquatic safety and is now a leader in the field. He is the president and founder of the Aquatic Safety Research Group and served as the director of aquatics and safety officer for athletics at Penn State University for nearly 25 years.

In 2000, Griffiths developed the *Five Minute Scanning Strategy* video that assists lifeguards in being more vigilant. The strategy is now required by all Pool Management Group, Star Guard, and Ellis & Associates Lifeguards. Griffiths has been published in over 300 scientific, professional, and popular journals. He has served as the president of the National Recreation and Park Association's National Aquatics Council. In 2008 he was inducted into the Pennsylvania Swimming Hall of Fame.

About the Contributors

B. Chris Brewster has served as president of the United States Lifesaving Association (www.usla.org) since 2003 and simultaneously as president of the Americas Region of the International Life Saving Federation (www.ilsf.org) and as a vice president of the ILS since 1983. He is a former lifeguard chief and harbormaster of the City of San Diego, California, with 22 years of service as a professional ocean lifeguard. He is a knight in the Order of Lifesaving of the ILS and the former lifesaving commissioner of the ILS, a life member of the United States Lifesaving Association, a life member of the California Surf Lifesaving Association, and a recipient of the International Swimming Hall of Fame Paragon Award for Aquatic Safety. Brewster is editor of *Open Water Lifesaving: The United States Lifesaving Association Manual* (2003), *The United States Lifesaving Association Manual of Open Water Lifesaving* (1995), *Guidelines for Open Water Lifeguard Training and Standards* (1993), and *Guidelines for Training and Standards of Aquatic Rescue Response Teams* (1996). He is a contributor to *Lifeguard Effectiveness: A Report of a Working Group*, published by the Centers for Disease Control and Prevention (2001), the *Handbook on Drowning* (2006), the *Encyclopedia of Coastal Science* (2005), and *Guidelines for Safe Recreational Water Environments*, issued by the World Health Organization (2005 and 2006). He is cofounder of the United States Lifeguard Standards Coalition. Brewster lectures on lifesaving matters internationally. He has a bachelor of science degree in journalism from the University of Colorado. Further information is available at www.lifesaver1.com.

Shawn DeRosa is the director of aquatics and safety officer for intercollegiate athletics at Pennsylvania State University. A nationally recognized expert in water safety, Shawn has been named by *Aquatics International* magazine as one of the top 25 people in the world of aquatics. Through DeRosa Aquatic Consulting, a water safety consulting firm, Shawn offers both education and training programs and consulting services to those involved in the field of aquatic recreation. Before joining Penn State, Shawn was the aquatics program coordinator for the Massachusetts state park system, where he oversaw 66 aquatic facilities, including 38 inland beaches, 20 swimming pools, and 6 ocean beaches. As an attorney, Shawn offers a practical understanding of risk management, which he incorporates in his many training sessions across the nation. He can be reached at www.derosaaquatics.com.

Andrew Mowen, PhD, is an associate professor in the department of recreation, park and tourism management at Pennsylvania State University. His research focused on the role of parks in shaping healthy lifestyles as well as funding strategies for parks and conservation areas. Dr. Mowen also teaches park administration and park facility planning courses for both undergraduate and graduate students. He has written extensively about the public's response to funding of park facilities and how parks contribute to public health goals. He has authored white papers for the United States Physical Activity Plan, the National Recreation and Park Association, and Active Living Research. Dr. Mowen currently serves as an associate editor for the *Journal of Park and Recreation Administration* and is a board member of the Pennsylvania Parks and Forests Foundation. He has a passion for the outdoors and is an avid bicyclist, angler, and hunter.

Robert E. Ogoreuc is assistant professor in the physical education department at Slippery Rock University and aquatic consultant for Aquatic Safety Resources. He also serves as aquatic director for the SRU physical education department overseeing the scheduling and operation of the lifeguards for academic classes. He earned his bachelor of science degree in health and physical education with an emphasis in aquatic administration at Indiana University of Pennsylvania (IUP) in 1989, and he earned his master of education degree in physical education and athletic administration at Slippery Rock University in 1996. He holds numerous certifications, including American Red Cross, WSI-IT, lifeguard instructor trainer, NAUI and SEI open water scuba instructor, EMT-B, and Pennsylvania fish and boat commission boating instructor. Mr. Ogoreuc has been the driving force in developing the Slippery Rock University aquatic minor. In 2008 and 2010, *Aquatic International* magazine recognized his efforts as one of the 25 Most Powerful People in Aquatics. He has also been recognized for his teaching efforts at SRU, where he received the William Herman Teaching Excellence Award in 2002 and 2004. In 2002 he participated as a scientific diver for the Cambrian Foundations Commodore Project. Mr. Ogoreuc has had the honor of working on the American Red Cross Water Safety Advisory Group that revised the water safety instructors' program in 2004. He has also worked as a technical reviewer for their lifeguard manuals. He has contributed to the United States Lifesaving Association, YMCA, and StarGuard lifeguard textbooks. He currently serves on the board of directors for the National Water Safety Congress and as president of the National Drowning Prevention Alliance. He also has made numerous presentations at the state, national, and international conferences.

Geoffrey Peckham chairs the American National Standards Institute's (ANSI) Standard for Environmental and Facility Safety Signs and has overseen critical updates for 2011. The new 2011 revision of the ANSI Z535.2 standard uses the latest risk assessment–based methodologies to define how best to warn about hazards involving potential injury or death and property damage. Since 1996, Peckham has chaired ANSI's U.S. technical advisory group to ISO/TC 145 (the international ISO standards committee responsible for global standardization of safety signs). Mr. Peckham will be a featured speaker at the National Drowning Prevention Alliance's 2011 National Drowning Symposium in Colorado Springs, Colorado. For more information about new developments in safety sign systems, contact Clarion at 800-748-0241 or e-mail info@clarionsafety.com.

Hans Vogelsong, PhD, is on the faculty at East Carolina University where he is the director of the coastal resources management PhD program within the Institute of Coastal Science and Policy. He also holds a position as associate professor in the department of recreation and leisure studies. Dr. Vogelsong has over 15 years of experience researching various facets of outdoor recreation participation and management. His most recent projects have centered on human dimensions of coastal and estuarine recreation and tourism. He has directed projects concentrating on an array of applied coastal-related subjects, including user conflicts, carrying capacity, economic impacts, satisfaction, user preferences for management alternatives, and minimizing depreciative behavior. His clients include the National Park Service, State of North Carolina, State of Delaware, U.S. Fish and Wildlife Service, NOAA, and several nonprofit agencies.

You'll find other outstanding recreation resources at
www.HumanKinetics.com

In the U.S. call 1.800.747.4457
Australia 08 8372 0999
Canada. 1.800.465.7301
Europe . . . . .+44 (O) 113 255 5665
New Zealand 0800 222 062

 HUMAN KINETICS
The Information Leader in Physical Activity & Health
P.O. Box 5076 • Champaign, IL 61825-5076